GREAT
GEORGIANS

The idea for GREAT GEORGIANS had its genesis in the years Zell Miller studied under the late Dr. E. Merton Coulter at the University of Georgia. From this great teacher, he learned that history is best told and best understood in terms of the larger-than-life personalities whose exploits comprise the struggles and achievements it chronicles.

It was while on the Athens campus that Miller began the research and notes which culminated a quarter of a century later in this volume bringing into focus the facts — many little known — about the motivations, labors, triumphs, failures, strengths, and weaknesses of the giants from Tomochichi to Jimmy Carter who are largely responsible for Georgia becoming what it is.

Premised upon the dreams of the English nobleman Oglethorpe, who was its founder, and the black preacher King, who became its conscience for a Georgia society based upon worth and effort instead of wealth and color, Miller paints bold word portraits of those Georgia leaders who both thwarted and advanced those dreams.

GREAT GEORGIANS blends their exciting personal histories into a rich and colorful historical tapestry of the total picture of Georgia's greatness in its Semiquicentenary Year.

Also by Zell Miller

THE MOUNTAINS WITHIN ME (1976)

Library of Congress Card Number 82-084745

GREAT
GEORGIANS

By
Zell Miller

First Printing — February 1983

Second Printing — March 1983

Published by

ADVOCATE PRESS

Franklin Springs, Georgia 30639

DEDICATION

This book is dedicated to my loyal Staff without whose ability and capacity for work I would be unable to pursue other activities and projects such as this.

Bill Burson

Mary Beazley
Donna Blankinship
Benny Bridges
Sarah Eby-Ebersole
Martha Gilland
Gigi Leverette
Elizabeth Martin
Marti Pingree

CONTENTS

Foreword 10

Hank Aaron 17

Ellis Arnall 21

Abraham Baldwin 25

Martha Berry 29

Joseph E. and Joseph M. Brown 34

Jimmy Carter 39

Elijah Clarke and John Clark 44

Ty Cobb 49

William H. Crawford 53

Lamar Dodd 57

Rebecca Latimer Felton 62

William Few 67

CONTENTS

Walter F. George 71

John B. Gordon 75

Henry W. Grady 79

Button Gwinnett 84

James and Joseph Habersham 88

Lyman Hall 93

Joel Chandler Harris 97

Nancy Hart 101

William B. Hartsfield 105

Benjamin Harvey Hill 110

James Jackson 114

Bobby Jones 119

Martin Luther King, Jr. 123

Sidney Lanier 128

Crawford W. Long 132

Juliette Gordon Low 137

Ralph McGill 141

CONTENTS

Margaret Mitchell 145

Ed Rivers 150

Dean Rusk 154

Richard B. Russell, Jr. 159

Sequoyah 164

John M. Slaton 169

Hoke Smith 173

Alexander H. Stephens 177

Eugene and Herman Talmadge 182

Tomochichi 186

Robert Toombs 190

Carl Vinson 195

George Walton 200

Thomas E. Watson 205

Robert W. Woodruff 209
    (including John S. Pemberton
    and Asa Griggs Candler)

Epilogue 214

FOREWORD

Two young men separated by two centuries and from two totally disparate backgrounds had two dreams and, in striving to realize them, made the State of Georgia what it has become in the 250 years of its sometimes momentous, often tumultuous, and always colorful existence.

Sir James Edward Oglethorpe, scion of a wealthy British aristocrat who forsook personal pleasure for public service, was horrified by the conditions of debtors in prison and the squalid, hopeless lives of the unemployed. He dreamed of establishing a colony in the New World where free and equal men, through their own labors, could build self-sufficient lives for themselves and their families.

Dr. Martin Luther King, Jr., a black preacher's son who forsook the peace of the pastor's study to brave police dogs, billy clubs, and fire hoses in the nonviolent pursuit of political, economic, and social equality, dreamed that "one day on the red hills of Georgia the sons of former slaves and the sons of former slaveowners will be able to sit down together at the table of brotherhood."

Oglethorpe personally led the hardy band of 114 hand-picked colonists in establishing the settlement of Savannah on Yamacraw Bluff and laid out the picturesque wards and squares which continue to characterize Old Savannah. He personally cemented the ties of friendship with Chief Tomochici and neighboring Indian tribes and personally commanded the troops who defeated the challenging Spanish from Florida in the Battle of Bloody Marsh. He personally encouraged the Jews, Salzburgers, Scotch Highlanders, French Huguenots, Moravians, and other freedom-loving and industrious refugees to settle in Georgia and personally kept slavery and rum out of the colony.

King personally galvanized the descendants of the slaves who were brought into the colony as soon as Royal Governors succeeded Oglethorpe and the original Trustees into a freedom force which could not be denied. From the bloody and tragic march on Selma, Alabama, the black freedom pioneers forged ahead to the monumental and triumphant march on Washington, D. C., the site of King's soul-stirring "I Have A Dream" speech which set the stage for the enactment of the historic Civil Rights Act of 1964 and culminated in his receiving the Nobel Peace Prize and his death by assassination.

It is mind-boggling to speculate how different the course of human history over the past 250 years might have been had any of the sequence of events and motivations which shaped the lives and destinies of the patrician Oglethorpe and the descendant-of-slaves King been different, especially had Oglethorpe been successful in keeping slavery permanently out of his beloved Colony of Georgia.

Two opposing forces were present in the colony from the beginning. On one hand, the cotton plantation economy produced wealth from the toil of black slaves. At the same time, the love of freedom and individual liberty was the legacy of the refugees from persecution who were the original colonists. Their Puritan-inspired successors grappled with these forces that generated the conflicts which propelled Georgia into the 250-year evolution from colony to revolution to independence to statehood to rebellion to reconstruction to industrialization to modernization to world leadership. The rise and demise of the first force led to the Civil War which produced the century-long struggle for the revitalization of the second. In short, during the course of two and a half centuries, Georgia has come the complete cycle from freedom to slavery to freedom, the distinguishing difference being that in the beginning the achievement of the fundamental right of free men and women to shape and achieve their own destinies was a goal and today it is an accomplished fact.

The history that was written during the course of those centuries is unparalleled in the drama of both its triumphs and its tragedies as well as in the magnitude of its human struggles and achievements. The saga is best told in terms of the larger-than-life personalities whose exploits comprised it.

The American Revolution produced many patriots but none more colorful than Joseph Habersham, the leader of the Liberty Boys who stole King George's ammunition in Savannah and sent it to the Minutemen for use in the Battle of Bunker Hill. Habersham later became Postmaster General in the Washington Administration. Another of these patriots was Button Gwinnett, the mysterious signer of the Declaration of Independence whose rare signature is a priceless collector's item. Gwinnett missed being the first governor of Georgia because of the opposition of the Scotch Highlanders of Darien whose leader later fatally wounded him in a duel. Certainly not to be omitted is Nancy Hart, the cross-eyed, red-haired backwoods Amazon who spied for the Patriots, fought with the troops of General Elijah Clarke, and personally captured and executed six Tories in an exploit which was questioned and discounted until their remains were unearthed by a railroad crew in 1912. And let us not forget Austin Dabney, a free black, who was wounded in the Battle of Kettle Creek (one of the few won by the Patriots in Georgia) after giving General Clarke another horse when the leader's was shot from under him in the fierce fighting.

It was during the early days of the Republic that the invention of the cotton gin by Eli Whitney in Georgia put King Cotton on his throne and higher education took on its first public dimension with Abraham Baldwin's establishment of the University of Georgia as the nation's first state-chartered university. States' rights first became an issue when Georgians questioned President Washington's direct negotiations with Alexander McGillivray for settlement of land disputes with the Indians on the Georgia frontier and the Chisholm case in which the State of Georgia was sued. The result was ratification of the Eleventh Amendment and the establishment of the doctrine of sovereign immunity of the states. A Georgian obtained the first patent for a steamboat and, although Robert Fulton was the first to build one, the first such vessel to cross the Atlantic departed from the port of Savannah in 1819 bearing the city's name. Dr. Crawford W. Long discovered the use of ether as an anesthetic for pain but failure to publish his finding caused his "first" to be disputed. Many Georgians fought for Texas independence and a Georgian, Mirabeau Lamar, was its second President. The Yazoo Land Fraud in which Georgia legislators tried to sell off the state's western lands became the nation's first and worst wholesale corruption of public officials until Watergate occurred seventeen decades later.

One of the greatest Georgians of all time was William Harris Crawford who served as both Secretary of War and of the Treasury in the Madison and Monroe administrations. Crawford would have become President in 1824 instead of John Quincy Adams but for a debilitating illness. It was at Crawford's Georgia home that he and President Monroe drafted the Monroe Doctrine. No other Georgian would come as close to being President until the election of Jimmy Carter in 1976. The only Georgian other than Dean Rusk ever to serve as Secretary of State was John Forsyth during the administration of Andrew Jackson. John McPherson Berrien also served as Attorney General under Jackson.

The most shameful chapter of Georgia's early history was the forcible removal of the highly-civilized Cherokee Nation to Oklahoma after the discovery of gold in North Georgia. On the infamous Trail of Tears, more than one-fourth of the 14,000 Cherokees who set out on the long journey perished. Within a quarter of a century, Georgians themselves were the objects of federal repression as General William Tecumseh Sherman cut a 60-mile-wide swath of scorched earth across the middle of the state on his devastating March to the Sea from Atlanta to Savannah. No state, before or since, has suffered the ravages of war as did Georgia in the Civil War.

Politics in Georgia developed factionally rather than along rigid party lines, giving the state its unique brand of intense and colorful parochial politics which pitted wealthy planters against poor farmers. Those divisions began with the contests between George M. Troup and John Clark (the son of Elijah who dropped the "e" so as not to appear ostentatious to his red-neck followers) before the Civil War and resumed with the machinations of the "Bourbon Triumvirate" of Joe Brown (followed by his son "Little Joe"), John B. Gordon, and Alfred Colquitt after Reconstruction. The development continued well past the mid-Twentieth Century with the pyrotechnics of Ole Gene Talmadge the father and Herman Talmadge the son. But for every firebrand there was a compensating statesman. Alexander Hamilton Stephens argued against secession, dutifully served as Vice President of the Confederacy, negotiated the termination of the conflict, and was restored to citizenship with the support of President Ulysses S. Grant, later becoming both United States Senator and Governor of Georgia. Hoke Smith fought the Browns, twice served as governor, and became Secretary of the Interior in the Cabinet of President Cleveland. John M. Slaton destroyed his political career by commuting the death sentence of Leo Frank because he did not believe the subsequently-lynched Jewish businessman to be guilty of the murder of Mary Phagan. Thomas W. Hardwick sacrificed his political future fighting the revival of the Ku Klux Klan and appointed the first woman to the United States Senate. Ellis Arnall sidetracked the rampaging demagoguery of Eugene Talmadge and set the stage for bringing blacks into the political mainstream. Finally there were three legislative

13

greats — United States Senators Walter F. George and Richard B. Russell and Congressman Carl Vinson — whose records of effective legislative service are unmatched before or since. They were perhaps the three most powerful men from Georgia to sit in the Halls of Congress. In a category all by himself and defying labeling is Thomas E. Watson, the erudite historian, incomparable orator, and father of Populism and Rural Free Delivery who flawed his potential greatness with virulent anti-Negro, anti-Catholic, and anti-Semitic writings and diatribes.

In the midst of all the political rhetoric and ferment, there were farsighted men like Henry W. Grady, the renowned Editor of **The Atlanta Constitution,** who made their voices heard over the nation as they sought to heal the wounds of war and to bring northern investment into the South to help build an industrial base on the ruins of cotton's kingdom. A series of expositions, most notably the Cotton States Exposition of 1895 in Atlanta, brought both visitors and money to the South and helped find markets for Georgia products as well as outlets for the talents of her people. An ex-Confederate General, John S. Pemberton, concocted the secret formula which Asa Candler and then Robert W. Woodruff merchandised to the world as Coca-Cola, starting countless fortunes which are the basis of much of Georgia's present-day prosperity and progressiveness.

The achievements of some of its women highlighted Georgia's economic rebirth. The redoubtable crusader for women's rights, Rebecca Latimer Felton, was the first woman to sit in the United States Senate, Walter George having delayed the presentation of his credentials of election for one day to permit her to take the oath. Juliette Gordon Low of Savannah founded the Girl Scouts. Alice McClellan Birney of Marietta established the National Conference of Parents and Teachers. Margaret Mitchell wrote **Gone With The Wind,** the most widely read and publicly acclaimed book since the Bible.

Georgia made its contribution in the area of sports records by producing the world's greatest golfer, the Grand Slam King Bobby Jones, and two of the world's foremost baseball greats. Ty Cobb earned the title "The Georgia Peach" by stealing bases, and Hank Aaron, the black slugger, broke Babe Ruth's all-time homerun record.

But none of these milestones to which we pointed with pride or events we preferred to forget had any frame of reference until the series of sociological earthquakes touched off by the school segregation decision of the United States Supreme Court in 1954 had run its course. After the overthrow of the infamous county unit system and the reapportionment of the Georgia General Assembly on the basis of population came the integration of public facilities, and later the triple assassinations of the Kennedy brothers and Martin Luther King. These upheavals resulted in Georgia's being forced into a modern society in which all men and women were equal in the opportunity to succeed or fail on the basis of their own talents and efforts rather than on the color of their skin, the place of their residence, or the size of their pocketbook.

The changes, though initially painful to many and still resisted by some, brought Georgia to the simultaneous realization of the dreams of Sir James Edward Oglethorpe and Dr. Martin Luther King, Jr., and, as a sentimentalist and a believer in a hereafter where good men and women reap the rewards of their efforts, I cannot help but believe that the two of them got together for some form of ecclesiastical celebration the day it all came into focus with the election of Georgia's Jimmy Carter as President of the United States.

— ZELL MILLER

Henry Louis "Hank" Aaron

(Baseball Player. Holder of 21 Major League Records, including Most Home Runs. Member Baseball Hall of Fame. Born February 4, 1934, Mobile, Alabama. Resides Atlanta, Georgia.)

When Hank Aaron was growing up playing sandlot baseball as a black kid in segregated Mobile, Alabama, he did not dream of becoming another Babe Ruth because, prior to 1947, playing in the major leagues was something those of his color could not do and, even with the pioneering done thereafter by Jackie Robinson, the idea seemed an "impossible" dream. In fact, he, like other black youths, had few dreams because the things to which he and his contemporaries could look forward were not the goals of which dreams were made. He was, however, a good athlete, playing star halfback on his high school football team, and began playing baseball with the semi-professional Mobile Black Bears during his junior year. That turned out to be his ticket out of the dead-end jobs he had held working in a fish market and an icehouse and mixing cement for bricklayers because, in an exhibition game at the age of seventeen, he caught the eye of the barnstorming Indianapolis Clowns and was offered $200 a month to play with them in the 1951 season. Looking back, Hank says he was "lucky" and in "the right place at the right time" because otherwise he probably would have been "stuck" in Mobile. As it happened, his controversial cross-handed batting style and .467 average drew the interest of scouts for the New York Giants and the Milwaukee Braves, and Hank chose the Braves because they offered him $200 more in the way of a bonus and a contract for $350 per month. The Clowns' owner received $10,000 for Hank's contract and gave him a cardboard suitcase as a going-away present.

Thus began a quarter of a century of a single-minded pursuit of baseball excellence by Henry Louis Aaron which caused many to call him an automaton, a cold fish, or worse, but he methodically added statistics to a growing record which likely never will be equalled. As an 18-year-old shortstop with the Braves' Eau Claire, Wisconsin, farm club in the Class C Northern League he batted .336 with nine home runs and 61 RBI's in 87 games and was named Rookie of the Year. The next year he moved up to the Jacksonville, Florida, Tars in the Class A South Atlantic League as a second baseman and was named the League's Most Valuable Player by batting a league-leading .362. He also led the League with 125 RBI's and hit 22 home runs in 137 games. At the same time he had a learning experience in racial prejudice or, as Hank put it, "I always knew there were prejudices . . . but for the first time I had a dose of it myself—name calling, threatening letters, staying at separate hotels. . . . I grew up a lot quicker than I ordinarily would have."

The Braves converted him to an outfielder and scheduled him to open the 1954 season with the Toledo, Ohio, team in the Class AAA American Association. When Bobby Thompson fractured his ankle in an exhibition game,, Hank was called to an early start on his illustrious 23-year major league career which rewrote baseball's hitting record book. Year after year he was one of the top hitters in the National League and, consequently, holds more major league batting records than any other player (21) and played in 24 Major League All-Star Games, including the years 1959-61 when two games were played. His amazing records include Most Games, Lifetime, 3,298; Most Runs Batted In, Lifetime, 2,297; Most Plate Appearances, Lifetime, 13,940; Most At-Bats, Lifetime, 12,364; Most Long Hits, Lifetime 1,477; and, of course, the one for which he is most renowned — Most Home Runs, Lifetime, 755. He is one of five players ever to hit more than 30 home runs and steal more than 30 bases in a season, doing it in 1963, and on May 17, 1970, he became the first player to compile both 3,000 career hits and more than 400 home runs. He was honored as the National League's Most Valuable Player in 1957 and was named Player of the Year by **Sporting News** in 1956 and 1963.

Aaron came to Atlanta with the transfer of the Braves' franchise in 1966. The most electrifying moment in his career came in the Atlanta-Fulton County Stadium on April 8, 1974, when he hit his 715th home run off the Dodgers' Al Downing to break what everyone had believed until about two years previously to be Babe Ruth's untouchable record. It was a moment in Georgia history which certainly has to rival the premier of "Gone With The Wind" and General Sherman's torching of Atlanta and one which established Hank "The Hammer" Aaron as a sports immortal. There may be those who contend that Hank's homers were shorter than the Babe's and that his record was achieved over a longer period of time, but such sour-grapes nit-picking is the one thing that can get Hank's usually unflappable nature aroused:

"You can't compare two ballplayers from different eras. . . . Some people say that I wasn't as good as Ruth because I went to bat more times than he did. But I could come back and say that I stole more bases in two seasons than he stole in 10; or that I won three gold gloves. What is the measure of a man's greatness? One man excels in one area, and one man excels in another.

"It's ridiculous, really, and sometimes I resent it. The people who saw Babe Ruth play say he hit those towering home runs that went forty rows in the stands, and I hit the ones that just barely made it over the fence. But, hey, we both touched four bases."

Traded to the Milwaukee Brewers, Hank went on to extend his record to 755 home runs before retiring at the end of the 1976 season and it is one which experts believe never again will be broken because of the tendency of today's players to take their big money and get out without going the long haul as Aaron did. His final home run, his 755th, came on July 20, 1976, in Milwaukee against California's Dick Drago. The last time he picked up a bat, in the Crackerjack Oldtimes Classic in Washington, D. C., in 1982, he fouled all five of the pitches he received, pitches which Hank himself admits "23 years ago I could have closed my eyes and hit them 40 rows back into the bleachers."

On August 1, 1982, Hank received the ultimate honor for a baseball player, induction into the Baseball Hall of Fame at Cooperstown, New York. His 714 ball and bat, his 3,000th base hit ball and bat, and his uniform and spikes had been enshrined there earlier. In the hallowed place where General Abner Doubleday invented the game in 1839, Henry Louis Aaron, in the presence of his beaming 82-year-old mother, with characteristic modesty joined his fellow Georgian Great Ty Cobb in baseball immortality with a soft-spoken, eight-minute speech devoted mainly to introducing his family and friends, paying tribute to the late Jackie Robinson as a man "who proved to the world that a man's ability is limited only by his lack of opportunity" and of his own career said, "It was not fame I sought, rather to be the best baseball player I could be."

Twenty days later the City of Atlanta unveiled a statue of Aaron at the stadium which was the scene of his greatest triumph and, at a later date, his 715 ball and bat will go on permanent display.

Hank now holds the position of Corporate Vice President of the Atlanta Braves, in which capacity he is in charge of the Braves' farm and player development programs. He also is devoting considerable time to work with the Boy Scouts, the programs of the NAACP, and worthy efforts to improve the lot of the poor. He and his second wife, Billye, are much in demand in social circles, and one of his five children who range in age from 27 to 15, son Lary, is an outfielder with the Braves' Bradenton Club in the Florida Rookie League.

Looking back over his career, Hank's greatest regret is that he didn't work harder to become a .400 hitter. He believes he could have, although he recognizes that his pursuit of the home run record caused him to become more of a pull hitter, thus reducing his prospects of increasing his overall batting average. Surprisingly, he does not regard the year he set his record as his greatest, choosing rather the year 1957 when "things seemed to come together for me" — the year that Milwaukee won the pennant and Hank was named the Most Valuable Player, leading the League with 118 runs, 44 homers, and 132 RBI's.

But unlike many of his predecessors and contemporaries, Hank does not like to talk about what he has done, saying he does not wish to "become an 'I' person."

"I got everything out of my ability that God gave me and more," he said, "I am completely satisfied."

The Atlanta Journal-Constitution summed up the significance of Aaron and his career upon the occasion of his Hall of Fame induction in these words:

"He has been an inspiration and a mentor to these young players as well as to many an Atlanta child. He is a leading citizen who contributes in many ways to many good causes. As a black star for the first major sports franchise in the Deep South, he opened many minds and hearts. His quiet dignity and self-respect contributed to the strength of the black people of the South. . . . On this particular day we share him with the world."

Ellis Gibbs Arnall

(Lawyer, Member and Speaker Pro Tempore of Georgia House of Representatives, Assistant Attorney General, Attorney General, Governor. Born March 20, 1907, Resides, Newnan, Georgia.)

Within the course of five momentous years Ellis Arnall played David to the Goliaths of both Eugene and Herman Talmadge, giving Ole Gene the political shellacking of his life at the polls and winning vindication from the courts after being forced out of office by "Hummon" and his followers in what he charged was a "coup d'etat." His courage, eloquence, and two successful books, along with the accomplishments of a progressive administration as governor which paid off the state debt without a tax increase, took stripes and chains off convicts, rewrote the cumbersome state constitution, and gave 18-year-olds the vote, brought him national acclaim as a liberal comer. But he never was able to translate into the higher office he coveted because his words and deeds failed to attract equivalent approval at home. By the time he attempted a political comeback twenty years later, he had become an anachronism who suffered the humiliation not only of losing the runoff to free-wheeling Lester Maddox, but also of failing to stop Maddox's election by a write-in campaign which threw the election into the General Assembly where Democrat Maddox was chosen over Republican Howard "Bo" Callaway.

A protege of Governor Ed Rivers under whom he served as Speaker Pro Tempore when he was Speaker of the House of Representatives, Arnall might never have gone higher than the office of Attorney General to which Rivers appointed him when a vacancy occurred had not the "Man from Sugar Creek" in his third term as Governor handed him a tailor-made issue.

This was Talmadge's racially-motived machinations which cost the institutions of the University System of Georgia their accredited standing. In his efforts to force the firing of Dean Walter D. Cocking of the University of Georgia College of Education and President Marvin S. Pittman of Georgia Teachers College at Statesboro because of their alleged advocacy of educational integration, Talmadge replaced three members of the Board of Regents and precipitated a purge of ten faculty members and the banning of twenty-three "subversive" textbooks from the public schools. The subsequent actions of accrediting agencies made Georgia degrees and diplomas worthless and touched off massive student demonstrations, including the hanging of Governor Talmadge in effigy on the grounds of the State Capitol. Arnall, calling Talmadge a "dictator" and accusing him of attempting to control education for "his own selfish ends," announced as a candidate against him when Talmadge sought reelection to a new unprecedented four-year term authorized by an amendment to the state constitution. Coupling his crusade against despotism at home at a time when the nation was locked in a death struggle against fascism abroad with the declaration that, if 18-year-olds were old enough to fight, they were old enough to vote, Arnall won an astounding landslide victory in both popular and county unit votes.

His administration was marked by one liberal success after another. In addition to making Georgia the first state to lower the voting age to eighteen, he was successful in repealing the poll tax, establishing a civil service system to give state employees their first protection against political firings, abolishing the last vestiges of the infamous "chain gang" penal system which had given Georgia a national black eye for many years, paying off the state debt without increasing taxes, and, through utilization of the mechanism of a commission instead of a convention, giving Georgia its first new state constitution since 1877. Included in the document were Articles on Home Rule and a State Merit System and a provision for independent, constitutional Boards of Regents and Pardons and Paroles, placing those sensitive functions out of political control for the first time in Georgia history. He failed, however, in his attempt to provide that a governor might succeed himself, the General Assembly overruling the Commission on that point. He personally argued the state's successful suit against discriminatory freight rates before the United States Supreme Court, wrote two books, **What The People Want** and **The Shore Dimly Seen,** and made many speeches throughout the country, some of which were criticized by Georgians as being derogatory to them and the South. The result was erosion of his popularity at home. He was widely mentioned as a possible vice presidential candidate, but President Roosevelt passed over him in favor of Senator Harry Truman. The closest Arnall ever came to holding national office was when Truman appointed him Director of the Office of Price Administration during the Korean War.

Barred from seeking reelection, Arnall turned his back on his old mentor Rivers and backed former State Representative James V. Carmichael as his successor, believing that the doubling of voter registration which had occurred during his term would put him in office. Rivers, however, ran anyway as a spoiler, and Talmadge, waging the most virulently racist campaign of his demagogic political career, managed to win a majority of the controlling county unit votes while losing in popular votes. The strain of the campaign proved too much for his frail health, however, and he died less than a month before assuming office, throwing the state into a crisis because of the silence of conflicting provisions governing succession under such circumstances. Arnall contended he would continue to hold office "until his successor shall be chosen and qualified." Talmadge backers, who had taken out the "insurance" of a write-in campaign for Talmadge's son, Herman, insisted the General Assembly should elect one of the two highest write-in candidates. The new Lieutenant Governor, Melvin E. Thompson, the state's first since colonial times, also claimed the office. The Legislature, however, elected Herman Talmadge who, with the support of Adjutant General Marvin Griffin and the control of the State Highway Patrol, proceeded to take over both the Governor's Office and Mansion by force when Arnall refused to surrender them and denounced Talmadge as "a pretender." Georgia's three-governor controversy, the second in its history, attracted international publicity and became a matter of litigation when Arnall resigned in favor of Thompson. Talmadge held the office for sixty-seven days until the Georgia Supreme Court ruled that Arnall's contention was correct and, inasmuch as he had resigned, Thompson would serve as Acting Governor until the next general election in which Talmadge defeated him decisively.

Arnall established one of the state's most lucrative law practices and made a large fortune representing Hollywood movie producers and in the insurance business. Though often rumored as a candidate for this or that office, he did not try to make a come back until 1966 when he ran in a lackluster primary against segregationist Lester Maddox and a bright newcomer, State Senator Jimmy Carter. His old-fashioned approach to campaigning and his quaint speaking style, however, created more mirth than support and he was defeated by Maddox in a runoff in which Republicans crossed over and voted for Maddox in the belief he would be the easiest for their candidate to beat in the general election.

Stung by that repudiation, Arnall allowed his name to be used in a write-in campaign staged largely by organized labor and pulled a sufficiently large vote to deny either Callaway or Maddox a majority. This threw the election into the General Assembly under that same provision which had figured in the three-governor controversy two decades earlier. The Legislature, being controlled by Democrats, chose Maddox, sensing an opportunity to achieve legislative dominance in the resulting power vacuum.

The former governor recently married for a second time following the death of his first wife. He continues to make his home in Newnan from which he commutes to his law offices in Atlanta.

Abraham Baldwin

(Scholar, Minister, Lawyer, Chaplain in Continental Army, Member Georgia House of Representatives, Founder and First President of University of Georgia, Member of Continental Congress, Signer of Constitution of United States, Member of first five Congresses, United States Senator, President Pro Tempore of United States Senate. Born November 8, 1784, Guilford, Connecticut. Died March 4, 1807, Washington, D. C.)

Abraham Baldwin was liked by everyone and is one of the very few political figures in Georgia history who was not controversial or criticized at one time or another. By every known account he was the "Mr. Nice Guy" of his time, a bachelor minister-lawyer who devoted himself to scholarship, public service, assisting deserving young men in obtaining educations, and supporting his orphaned stepbrothers and stepsisters. The poet Joel Barlow, his brother-in-law and admirer, said he "lived without reproach and probably died without an enemy." His fellow United States senators who had elected him Senate President Pro Tempore stayed in Washington two days past adjournment and braved a storm to attend his final rites and interment, one of their number later writing "never did I see such solemnity and regret."

Had the term then been current, Baldwin probably would have been the subject of jokes about the "Yale Mafia" because it was in concert with three of his fellow Yale alumni that he was the prime mover in the establishment of the University of Georgia as the nation's first state-chartered university. The idea for the University was first broached by Yaleman Lyman Hall while Governor, and he and Baldwin were the principal authors of the charter which was granted two years later. Another Yale-educated physician and former governor, Dr. Nathan Brownson, worked with them in getting the grant of 40,000 acres approved by the General Assembly for the support of the University. A fourth Yale alumnus, Dr. Josiah Meigs, was persuaded by Baldwin to come to Georgia and succeed him as President when Baldwin was elected to the United States Senate. He also was responsible for bringing another Connecticut educator to Georgia — David Bushnell — inventor of the submarine, who taught school in Columbia County and settled in Warrenton as a "Doctor of Physics."

Baldwin was a prodigy who was admitted to Yale at the age of fourteen and graduated at the age of eighteen and immediately employed as a tutor and later a professor. He also studied theology and law and served as a chaplain in the Continental Army where he came to the favorable attention of General Nathanael Greene. It was on Greene's recommendation that he moved to Georgia in 1784 where his rise to prominence was nothing short of phenomenal. He was admitted to the bar within six days of the filing of his petition on January 14, 1784, was granted 200 acres of land in Wilkes County on October 22 of the same year, and was elected the following January to represent that county in the State Legislature. From that time until his death he was in the active service of his state and nation.

His first act in the General Assembly was the drafting, with the help of Doctors Hall and Brownson, of the charter for a state-supported university which was approved on January 27, 1785, making Georgia the first state in the Union to so act. He was then elected a delegate to the Continental Congress and to the United States Constitutional Convention where he, along with William Few, was one of the two Georgians to sign that document. He is credited, along with other friends from Connecticut, with working out the compromise between large and small states which made it possible for the smaller ones to ratify the new Constitution without fear of their being dominated by the big states in the Congress.

He was active in seeking ratification of the Constitution by Georgia and was elected, as a Federalist, to the First Congress and the four subsequent Congresses. He was elected to the United States Senate in 1799 and reelected in 1805. His great regret in going to Washington was that he had to leave the

Presidency of the University of Georgia before getting its classes underway. His fellow senators gave him the highest office they could bestow by electing him their President Pro Tempore, third in the line of succession to the Presidency, on December 7, 1801. He was joined in the Senate in 1801 by his good friend, General James Jackson. The two served as a close and effective team. It was Baldwin who was sitting with Jackson when he died, and it was Baldwin who announced his death to the Senate "with tears in his eyes." So wrote John Quincy Adams. Baldwin died one year later and was buried by Jackson's side in the Old Congressional Cemetery in Washington. His remains have been moved twice, first to the Barlow Estate and later to Rock Creek Cemetery where they rest today under a simple marker.

Baldwin was not wealthy and lived frugally on his congressional salary of six dollars a day. Nevertheless, he was generous in providing assistance to deserving young men who sought an education. Young Alexander Hamilton Stephens who was to become Vice President of the Confederacy was one of his beneficiaries. After the death of his father, who had been widowed and married again when Baldwin was in college, he contributed substantially to the education and support of his six stepbrothers and stepsisters. His portrait was painted by another of his famous friends, Robert Fulton, builder of the first steamboat. Upon Baldwin's death, the members of the Georgia General Assembly wore mourning bands on their arms and immediately adopted a resolution creating a county named in his honor. This county was to become the site of the new State Capitol with its capital city being named for another of Baldwin's friends, also a benefactor of the University of Georgia, John Milledge. In later years, a unit of the University System of Georgia at Tifton would be named in his honor.

Although a Federalist in belief and practice, Baldwin was not so rigid and doctrinaire in his views that he was intolerant of those of others. The National Portrait Gallery of Distinguished Americans states of him in its fourth edition:

"His manner of conducting business was worthy of the highest commendation; he may have wanted ambition to make himself brilliant, but he never wanted industry to make himself useful. His oratory was simple, forcible, convincing. His maxim of never asserting anything but what he believed to be true could not fail to be useful in carrying conviction to others. Patient of contradiction, and tolerant to the wildest opinions, he could be as indulgent to the errors of judgment in other men as if he had stood the most in need of such indulgence for himself."

His biographer, Dr. Charles C. Jones, Jr., further traces his course in achieving acclaim in congressional service:

"So manly was his course in Congress and in the Senate of the United States, so conservative were his views, so conscientious was his conduct in the discussion of all constitutional questions, and so steadfast his adherence to what he conceived to be the cardinal principles of government, that he acquired and retained in a wonderful degree the confidence of the party to which he was attached, the respect of those who held different notions with regard to the political questions which then agitated the country, and the approbation of his constituents. Of him it has been truthfully said that he 'died with the consciousness of having faithfully and fearlessly filled the measure of his public duties.' "

Martha McChesney Berry

(Educator, Philanthropist, Founder of the Berry Schools. Born October 7, 1866, near Rome, Georgia. Died February 27, 1942, Atlanta, Georgia.)

The mountain people around Rome, Georgia, called her the "Sunday Lady of Possum Trot" and the story of how Martha McChesney Berry came by that appellation of awe, respect, and love is worthy of the most imaginative writer of scripts for the silver screen. She was born into a life of wealth and privilege in the aftermath of the Civil War, was educated by private tutor and in Mme. LeFebvre's exclusive Edgeworth School of Baltimore, traveled extensively in Europe. Had she so chosen, her life could have been that of a debutante and society matron in the most fashionable circles of national society. But she opted to spend it instead in providing an educational opportunity for the pitiful poor and benighted children of Appalachia. In so doing, she founded and developed one of the greatest educational institutions of its kind and pioneered a form of work-study which has been emulated throughout the world.

Martha Berry came into her life's work quite by accident. She had returned to her family home near Rome following the completion of her studies and travels with the ambition of becoming a writer. She set up a study and den in the log-cabin playhouse on her father's plantation where she and her five sisters and two brothers had been tutored by Miss Ida McCullough. While sitting there one Sunday afternoon pondering possible subjects for her writings, she heard children's voices in the woods outside. Upon investigating, she found three boys in ragged homespun overalls whom she invited inside to have some apples. As they ate, she told them some Bible stories and was so impressed by their rapt attention that she questioned them about their lives. She was shocked to learn that their deprivation was even more abject than she had imagined and that there was not even a school available for them to attend. She resolved then and there to do something about it and invited the boys to return the following Sunday.

Return they did, and soon they were bringing not only their brothers, sisters, and friends but also their parents and neighbors. Everyone would gather around Miss Berry and listen in almost worshipful silence as she taught them from the Bible in scenes which must have been reminiscent of those in which Jesus was depicted relating the parables to his disciples and followers. Because the Sunday School quickly outgrew Martha's cabin, she moved the sessions into the old church of the nearby community known as Possum Trot. As the popularity of the sessions grew, she opened satellite classes in Mount Alto and Foster's Bend on Sundays. On weekdays, she began driving her buggy into the remote settlements and to isolated individual mountain homes. On those trips she would carry her melodeon with her and, in addition to telling stories, would teach hymns to the music-loving mountain people who delighted in singing with her. The fame of the "Sunday Lady of Possum Trot" spread across the ridges, valleys, and coves until she was known not only in all the surrounding counties but as far away as Alabama and Tennessee.

The idea of a regular school in which she could add the three r's of reading, 'riting, and 'rithmetic to that of religion already was actively forming in her mind when a young mountain lad she had not seen before presented himself at her cabin and declared, "Here I am, ma'am, come ter git l'arnin'." She immediately began talking with the men and boys in her Sunday Schools and they agreed to contribute their carpentry skills if she could provide the materials needed to build a schoolhouse. Taking $1,000 of her inheritance, which at that time was a small fortune, she bought the lumber, nails, brick, and other necessities which her pupils fashioned into a white-washed schoolhouse across the road from her home. This road is now known as the Martha Berry Highway (U. S. Route 27). That was an improvement, but Martha was dissatisfied with the results. Attendance was sporadic at best, depending upon the weather and the demands of planting and harvesting the yearly cotton and corn crops. So in 1902 she decided to build a dormitory and open a boarding school for boys where they would work to pay their expenses.

By that time many of her wealthy friends were beginning to believe that she had lost her mind and tried to dissuade her from the course on which she was set. But she was able to convince Judge Moses Wright of the need and wisdom of her project, and he assisted her in deeding eighty-three of the acres of land she had inherited for establishment of the Boys Industrial School. Judge Wright agreed to become one of its first trustees. She named the entrance to the school the "Gate of Opportunity" by which it is known to this date. Thus was born the institution we know today as the Berry Schools, a complex composed of a middle school, academy, and college with a campus of 28,000 acres of scenic forests, fields, mountains, lakes, and streams. Almost 2,000 students from throughout the world are served by the Berry Schools in an academic environment acclaimed for its excellence and from which no student is ever turned away for lack of resources. From the beginning the program was one of balanced emphasis on learning, working, and worshiping, and it continues so today. Berry graduates are much sought after by employers because of the schools' demonstrated belief in the work ethic, academic excellence, and moral values.

Miss Berry proved as adept in persuading the wealthy of the nation to open their hearts and purses to her schools as she was in winning the hearts and devotion of her mountain proteges. She talked Andrew Carnegie into a $50,000 endowment if she could match it, which she did, and charmed President Theodore Roosevelt not only into giving a dinner party for her at the White House and introducing her to many of his wealthy friends but also into visiting the campus and giving his personal approval to her programs. "This is one of the greatest practical works for American citizenship that has been done within this decade," she told the President. Perhaps her greatest and most profitable conquests were Mr. and Mrs. Henry Ford who also visited the campus. The automobile magnate and his wife wound up giving tractors to the farm, buying large new tracts of land for the school, and building the magnificent Gothic Ford Center with its classrooms and auditorium which is the heart of today's campus and a favorite of visiting shutterbugs.

By 1907 there were 150 boys earning their educations in the boarding school. Two years later with the encouragement of President Roosevelt but against other well-meaning advice, a girls' division was opened. In fact, Miss Berry often joked that if she had known in the beginning how much work girls could do and how much boys would eat she probably would have begun with girls instead. Further, during World War II, girls took over all the men's jobs at the schools and proved they

31

could carry on all aspects of the program while the men were away fighting.

In response to the need for teachers, Berry Junior College was opened in 1926 and a full four-year college graduated its first class in 1932. By the time of the Great Depression, it was possible for a student to work his way through high school and college at Berry. After World War II and following Miss Berry's death in 1942, her successors led by then Chairman of the Federal Reserve System William McChesney Martin, Jr., and Georgia's renowned banker and attorney, John A. Sibley, made some changes. A modern graduate program was instituted, the faculty was upgraded, and the college generally was placed on an academic level with any comparable institution of higher learning in the world. Miss Berry would have been particularly pleased that its presidency when last filled went to a highly-respected female educator, Dr. Gloria Shatto.

Miss Berry devoted her life to the development and support of her schools. She traveled the world over to obtain gifts and endowments for them. Nothing escaped her attention; she was interested in everything, from the dairy herd and barns to the scientific laboratories. She insisted that steeples be placed on all the buildings, including the chicken houses, to emphasize her belief that work well done is the truest form of worship of God.

She received many honors. The University of Georgia conferred an honorary Ph. D. degree upon her as did eight other major institutions of higher learning. The Georgia General Assembly in 1924 adopted a resolution giving her distinguished citizenship. In 1925 she was awarded the Roosevelt Medal for services to the nation. She was widely acclaimed as a lecturer. Even her ambition to become a writer was realized through publication of **The Southern Highlander,** a magazine, issued under the direction of the Berry Schools, which attracted many favorable reviews for its articles on Southern mountain people.

Her death in Atlanta on February 27, 1942, occasioned national mourning and an outpouring of tributes to her life and accomplishments. **The San Francisco Examiner** called her "a true patriot who gave her life for her country." **The Miami Herald** wrote, "It is harder to live for one's country than to die for it, and America so needs a few more patriots like Martha Berry to stand by it."

Perhaps the greatest tribute of her entire career came from the taciturn and usually undemonstrative President Calvin

Coolidge who said to her, "In building out of nothing a great educational institution for the children of the mountains you have contributed to your time one of its most creative achievements."

Joseph Emerson Brown (Father)

(Lawyer, State Senator, Judge, Four-Term and Civil War Governor, Chief Justice of Georgia Supreme Court, United States Senator, President of Atlanta Board of Education, Trustee of University of Georgia for 32 years, Industrialist, Philanthropist. Born April 15, 1821, near Pickens, South Carolina. Died November 30, 1894, Atlanta, Georgia.)

Joseph Mackey "Little Joe" Brown (Son)

(Scholar, Lawyer, Railroad Commissioner, twice Governor. Born December 18, 1851, Cherokee County, Georgia. Died March 3, 1932, Marietta, Georgia.)

The fiction of Horatio Alger pales by comparison with the true facts of the rise of Joseph Emerson Brown from poverty and illiteracy in the North Georgia Mountains to become one of the wealthiest and most powerful and controversial leaders in Georgia history. For almost four decades he so dominated the Georgia political scene that few events preceding, during, and following the Civil War could be recorded without mention of his participation or influence.

With the exception of the Reconstruction years, during two

34

of which he served by appointment as Chief Justice of the Georgia Supreme Court, there was not a time between 1857 and 1897 that one of the "Bourbon Triumvirate" — of which he was a principal with Alfred H. Colquitt and John B. Gordon — was not serving as either Governor or United States Senator. His son, Joseph Mackey "Little Joe" Brown, served twice as governor after the turn of the century. His record of serving four successive terms as Governor never will be equalled unless the state constitution is changed. It is, therefore, most fitting that his unique record of service is commemorated by an unique husband-and-wife statue on the southwest lawn of the State Capitol.

It hardly seems possible that the stern, bearded, affluent patriarch of that statue is the same individual as the gangling, barefoot lad of nineteen who walked a yoke of steers from Gaddistown in Union County as payment for his first eight months of formal schooling at Calhoun Academy in South Carolina. Or the earnest scholar who conducted his own school by day, read law by night, and tutored the children of a physician to earn the tuition to Yale Law School. Or the shy, tongue-tied lawyer who so impressed his neighbors in Cherokee County that they elected him first to the State Senate and then Judge of the Blue Ridge Circuit.

The image also is far removed from that of the 36-year-old judge who was in the field on his farm scything and binding wheat when he was chosen without his knowledge or consent to be the Democratic nominee for Governor. This action took place on the 21st ballot of a deadlocked State Convention in a deal worked by the delegates from Cherokee County with Linton Stephens, brother of "Little Aleck," who was chairman of the Convention's Compromise Committee. Or that of the pale, awkward, and inarticulate campaigner who had to be coached on the techniques of platform debate by Robert Toombs but who managed to best his silver-tongued American Party opponent, Benjamin Harvey Hill, by identifying with his constituency and speaking their language.

Hill's undoing proved to be his characterization of Brown as "slow" and by making fun of a quilt which a group of mountain women presented him as a campaign contribution. The newspapers took up the cause of the quilt, one in Milledgeville editorializing: "Hurrah for the girls of Cherokee, the plough boy judge and the calico quilt!"

Brown established himself with the common people by responding, "I'm a slow man and proud of it. Any man who holds in his hands the destinies of his people must be cautious and slow to act." No darker horse in any campaign ever won a more clear-cut victory, Brown triumphing over Hill 56,568 to 46,826.

Brown proved himself a different breed of cat from his first day in office, taking on the banks and special interests on the issue of suspension of specie payment during the Recession of 1857 (a fight which he lost) and championing the cause of public education by advocating the earmarking of rentals from the Western and Atlantic Railroad for that purpose (a fight which he won). On national issues he was a Calhounist, believing first, last, and always in states' rights. On state issues he was a Jacksonian activist, so much so that his followers began calling him "Young Hickory."

His popularity was such that he was reelected by a landslide. In his second term he proved his foresight by seeking and getting an appropriation of $1 million to recruit and equip an expanded and reformed State Militia, making Georgia the best prepared of the Confederate States when the Civil War erupted.

Brown was an ardent secessionist who joined the Breckinridge faction of the Democratic Party despite the fact that Georgian Hershel V. Johnson was the Vice Presidential nominee of the Douglas faction. Governor Brown ordered the seizure of unoccupied Fort Pulaski at the entrance to Savannah Harbor before the firing on Fort Sumter and took over the Federal Arsenal at Augusta and the Federal Mint at Dahlonega immediately thereafter. From the start he had reservations about the Confederacy, proving himself to be as big a states' rights thorn to Jefferson Davis as he and other Southern leaders ever were to Abraham Lincoln. Brown, Stephens, and Toombs fought Davis over such issues as conscription, martial law, impressment of property, control of the State Militia, peace negotiations, and the entire spectrum of issues confronting the Richmond government. The three laid most of the blame for the failure of the Confederacy at Davis' doorstep.

Brown did not want a third term and refused to campaign for one, but was reelected handily. Not surprisingly, he took the oath of office wearing a suit of Georgia-made jeans. His genius for organization and management came to the fore in mobilizing and expanding Georgia's growing industrial base, transforming the state into the arsenal and breadbasket of the Confederacy.

Governor Brown insisted upon maintaining a State Militia. Every time Richmond called up more Georgia troops, he recruited younger and older Georgians until in the latter days of the war he had a State Guard mainly of military school students, including his own son, and old men. When there were no rifles available, he armed some of them with spears known as "Joe Brown's Pikes."

He accused Jefferson Davis of complicity in the effort to unseat him in 1863, but won a fourth term on the strength of absentee ballots from Georgia fighting men on the battle-fronts. He was presiding over a special session of the legislature trying to figure out ways to organize and finance further fighting units when the war ended. He was arrested and briefly incarcerated in Washington, D. C., until he was pardoned by President Johnson on the strength of certain promises: that he would return to Georgia, that he would resign as Governor, and that he would advocate citizen acceptance of the war's end and the conditions of Reconstruction.

It was the latter course which transformed him from the most loved into the most hated Georgia political figure. In July 1868 at the largest mass meeting ever held until that time —referred to as "The Bush Arbor Meeting" — he was given a "savage" denunciation "greeted with deafening applause" which resulted in the only political defeat of his career. The General Assembly subsequently elected Joshua Hill United States Senator over him. Reconstruction Governor Rufus Bullock then appointed Brown to a 12-year-term as Chief Justice of the Georgia Supreme Court, but he resigned in two years to head up the company which leased the Western and Atlantic Railroad. He then began to accumulate the fortune which was to make him a multi-millionaire before his death and probably the richest Georgian of his time. He expanded his business and industrial interests into real estate, iron and coal mining and various manufacturing enterprises. His companies became involved in the infamous Georgia convict-leasing system to the extent that at one time he offered to lease the entire available prison population for twenty years for $25,000 a year. This brought much criticism.

But his burning ambition was to vindicate his reputation with the people and to resume public service. Such an opportunity came in 1880 when John B. Gordon resigned as Senator to take a high-paying railroad job. Governor Colquitt appointed Brown to succeed Gordon in a switch which touched off charges of "bargain and corruption." But Brown made good use of the position and recouped popular acclaim by leading the fight to defeat legislation to deny Mexican War pensions to men who subsequently fought for the Confederacy. He was reelected to a full term in his own right and, in a career-climaxing irony, served as junior Senator to his first major political adversary, Benjamin Harvey Hill. After the conclusion of his term, he devoted the remainder of his life to his business interests, to serving the cause of education as a Trustee of the University of Georgia and President of the Atlanta Board of Education, his work as an active Baptist layman and his philanthrophies. Among these were an endowment for the Southern Baptist Theological Institute and the establishment of a loan fund for deserving needy young men to attend the University of Georgia.

Brown did not live to see his son become Governor, although he would have relished "Little Joe's" victory in challenging and defeating Governor Hoke Smith who had fired **him** as a Member of the State Railroad Commissioner to which **he** had been appointed by Governor Joseph Terrell. With the help of the Old Warrior Tom Watson, who had broken with Smith over his refusal to commute the death sentence of a Watson follower, "Little Joe" defeated Smith on economic issues growing out of the Depression of 1907 with a slogan, "Hoke and Hunger, Brown and Bread." In the campaign he refused to make any speeches and promised that, if elected, he would perform the duties of the office and "not be found running all over the State for weeks at a time and allowing the business of his office to take care of itself."

"Little Joe" was a scholarly young man who graduated with honors from Oglethorpe University with a 99.5 average and later had to give up a promising brilliant law career because of weak eyesight. He was narrowly defeated for reelection by Smith, but won in a special election to complete the term when Smith was elected to a vacancy in the United States Senate shortly after his inauguration. Although his contests with Smith were two of the fiercest and most divisive in Georgia history, "Little Joe" as Governor never was able to strike the spark of public adoration that his father achieved twice in his career. Uninterested in continuing the reform efforts of his predecessor, his administrations were generally quiet and undistinguished. His political career ended in 1914 when he unsuccessfully opposed Smith for reelection to the Senate.

In many respects the dual careers of the Browns parallel those of the Talmadges, Eugene and Herman, who followed them. But none attained the heights of Joseph Emerson Brown on whose tomb these appropriate words are inscribed: "His history is written in the annals of Georgia."

James Earl "Jimmy" Carter, Jr.

(Nuclear Physicist, Naval Officer, Peanut Farmer, School Board Member, State Senator, Governor, President of the United States. Born October 1, 1924. Resides, Plains, Georgia.)

It will be for the historians of the future to judge whether the Presidency of Jimmy Carter was flawed and, if so, whether the blame rests with him, his traits of character, the failings and inadequacies of his subordinates, or the cannibalistic tendency of today's electorate to debase and devour those it honors with high office. From a current perspective it would appear that while Carter inflicted some unnecessary wounds upon himself, the tough issues which confronted him during his four years in office — ranging from energy to inflation and the Panama Canal to the Iranian hostages — were no-win matters from which not even a Franklin Delano Roosevelt could have wrung political advantage.

Considering the mood of an affluent nation facing up to a future of lowered expectations and the intransigence of a Congress paralyzed by fear of the power of militant one-issue constituencies, Carter accomplished as much as could have been expected of any President under the circumstances. Further, he probably attempted to do more than most of his detractors would have dared had they been in his shoes in the same situations. But all of that is immaterial to the central point of the historical and sociological significance of the Carter Presidency and that is that his election as a Deep Southerner ended for all time the second-class citizenship of people in the states of the Old Confederacy and marked the true realization of a national citizenship which transcends the previous barriers of race and geography. Jimmy Carter, by his candidacy and election, made the United States truly what its citizens always pledged themselves to be, "One Nation, under God, indivisible with liberty and justice for all," and made reality of both the vision of Sir James Edward Oglethorpe and the dream of Martin Luther King, Jr.

No President ever brought to the office the qualifications which Carter did. As a peanut farmer, his roots were in the agriculture which had made America great, and, as a nuclear physicist, his life's work had been in the high technology to which America looked to keep it great. An intense and studious, almost introverted loner, he grew up in one of the most conservative and racially-conscious counties of Southwest Georgia. There he learned the satisfactions of hard work and public service from a driving father and inherited the dreams of a visionary from his free-spirited mother, a nurse who proved her independence by going to India with the Peace Corps after she was widowed. His boyhood idol was Senator Richard B. Russell, Jr., who appointed him to the U. S. Naval Academy after he had studied for a year each at Georgia Southwestern College and Georgia Tech. After two years with the Pacific Fleet, he applied for Submarine School, was sent to Union College to study nuclear physics, and became a protege of Admiral Hyman Rickover when assigned to the pre-commissioning crew of the nation's second nuclear submarine, the *USS Seawolf.* The relationship with Rickover continued into his Presidency when he saved the Admiral from enforced retirement due to age and often sought his advice on matters of defense.

Carter had resigned his commission as a full Lieutenant in 1953 upon the death of his father to return to Plains to take over the family peanut business. He was elected to the Sumter County School Board where he became embroiled on the side of moderation in the school integration controversy. In 1962 he ran for the State Senate in a race characterized by fraudulent balloting which counted him out. But with the help of Atlanta Attorney Charles Kirbo who later was to become his most trusted and intimate adviser and confidant, he succeeded in overturning the results and took his seat for the first of two terms in that body.

Carter's surprisingly-strong third-place finish in the 1966 Democratic primary for governor, which probably cost Ellis Arnall the nomination and set the stage for Lester Maddox's ultimate election by the General Assembly, established him as a bright, new face on the Georgia political scene. In a four-year campaign in which he and his wife Rosalynn shook the hand of virtually every voter in the state, he defeated Former Governor Carl Sanders for the office in 1970 in a bitter race which made the two unrelenting political enemies. In his inaugural address as the state's new Governor Carter made national headlines and the cover of **Time Magazine** with his declaration that "the time for racial discrimination is over," becoming the first Georgia chief executive to so affirm racial equality.

He dedicated the first two years of his administration to duplicating the feat of Dick Russell in reorganizing state government and waged a tumultuous but successful two-year battle to reduce the number of state agencies from more than 300 to thirty. Included in the reorganization was abolition of the elected office of State Treasurer and the establishment of a monster welfare and health agency known as the Department of Human Resources. In addition he implemented a computer-age system of finance known as "Zero Base Budgeting." His relations with the legislature in general and Lieutenant Governor Lester Maddox in particular crippled his legislative programs during his last two years in office. While he was successful in getting a campaign financial disclosure law enacted, he failed in his major effort for consumer protection legislation.

His popularity had eroded considerably by the time his term ended and the subsequent announcement of his presidential candidacy was greeted with expressions of incredulity and derision. But with the help and advice of Hamilton Jordan, a young political genius who was Carter's Executive Secretary when he was Governor and would become his Chief of Staff as President, he applied to the national campaign the same techniques of assiduous personal campaigning he had used in Georgia. Beginning with his success in the Iowa caucuses, he soon made believers of even the most skeptical national pundits. Sophisticated Washington never had seen the likes of the Carters and, from the day of the inauguration when he and Rosalynn walked the parade route to the White House, they did not fit the mold of the establishment. Their informal and unpretentious life-style, including the banning of hard liquor from White House functions, brought them increasing criticism and ostracism.

Carter tackled the Presidency with the same totality of commitment and effort that characterized his governorship. Yet he was criticized for too many initiatives in too many areas and for failing to court the support of Congress. He was especially derided for his ambitious energy program which he declared to be "the moral equivalent of war," for eliminating the trappings of presidential pomp and power, for holding barbecues instead of state dinners, for wearing sweaters instead of coats, and for insisting upon knowing every detail and dotting every "i" and crossing every "t" in every program and initiative of the federal government. His single-mindedness of purpose did pay off in one particular instance, however, and that was the success of the Camp David accords in which he literally wore down Egyptian President Sadat and Israeli Prime Minister Begin into signing a peace agreement. This document went far toward defusing the volatile Middle Eastern situation. The opposite was the result in the Iranian crisis in which he succeeded only in imprisoning himself in the White House. One of his deepest disappointments was being denied the satisfaction of seeing the American hostages released during his term of office.

During his reelection campaign, the traits which won for him four years earlier turned into what Jordan characterized in his book **Crisis** as "the meanness issue." The incumbent President came across as beating up on a father figure while Ronald Reagan "aw-shucked" his way around his lack of knowledge on the problems confronting the country. As Jordan explained the loss, Reagan projected the image of a comfortable conservative who inspired trust while Carter "had no unifying political philosophy," having wrestled with each issue of his Presidency and an **ad hoc** and often expedient basis. The antics and escapades of his brother Billy, and other members of his real and political families also proved damaging to the public's confidence in him. A further irony was the fact that his upfront, "Born Again" religious faith which drew the support of voters looking for a restoration of morality in government in his first race did not wear well. In fact, it turned off voters at both ends of the spectrum in his second, both those who objected to the religious undertones of his actions and those rigid fundamentalists who felt he was not committed strongly enough to issues such as banning abortion and returning prayer to public classrooms.

Following his defeat, he returned to Plains where he mastered a word processor and wrote his memoirs, **Keeping Faith.** He further immersed himself in the establishment of a Presidential Library and Policy Center on a site adjacent to the Emory University Campus in Atlanta. Even in that pursuit, controversy did not escape him. The land he proposed to use for his library and a network of access roads was the same property on which he had stopped construction of a four-lane freeway during his administration as Governor. The same people who persuaded him to take that action objected to the roads and traffic his memorial center would entail.

Elijah Clarke (Father)

(Pioneer Settler, Indian Fighter, Hero of American Revolution, Major General of Georgia Militia. Born 1733, Edgecombe County, North Carolina. Died January 15, 1799, Wilkes County, Georgia.)

John "Jack" Clark* (Son)

(Hero of American Revolution, Major General of Georgia Militia, State Legislator, Political Leader of Small Farmers, twice Governor of Georgia, Indian Agent for Florida Territory. Born 1766, Edgecombe County, North Carolina. Died October 15, 1842, St. Andrews, Florida. Reinterred Marietta National Cemetery.)

British and Indians alike learned painfully why the area of Old Wilkes County was called "The Hornet's Nest" because they were stung badly by Elijah Clarke and his fighting family and followers every time they tried to conquer it. In fact, the British never were able to establish control over there as they did in most of the rest of Georgia during the American Revolution. Although he did not achieve the fame of his South

---

*John Clark elected to drop the "e" from the family surname so he would not appear ostentatious to his red-neck followers.

Carolina compatriot, Francis (The Swamp Fox) Marion, Elijah Clarke forced the British and their American sympathizers, called Tories, to expend considerable effort, manpower, and material trying to keep him in check.

The Battle of Kettle Creek, fought on War Hill about eight miles from Washington, Georgia, was one of the few decisive victories won by the Georgia Patriots. Clarke and his men were able to accomplish this feat in a surprise attack at dawn, carried out on the basis of information supplied the General by his friend and neighbor, Nancy Hart. It was a bloody encounter in which the British commander, Colonel Thomas Boyd, was fatally wounded; Clarke's 13-year-old son, John, was a hero; and the free black, Austin Dabney, was wounded and later rewarded for bravery and for providing Clarke with a replacement horse when his own was shot from under him.

When the Revolution began, Clarke, who had moved into the area from Edgecombe County, North Carolina, already was the Captain of a body of horsemen he had assembled to protect the area from marauding Indians. He was wounded for the first of four times when his unit participated in the abortive expedition led against St. Augustine by General Howe. He evacuated the women and children of the area to Watauga Valley, North Carolina, although his wife, Hannah, and their eight children along with Nancy Hart and her family chose to stay and fight. Clarke fought Scotch Colonel Innes at Wofford's Iron Works, capturing 100 and killing sixty-three Redcoats at Musgrove's Mill. In the latter battle, he was wounded twice, his life being saved by his stock-buckle which deflected what otherwise probably would have been a fatal bullet. His riflemen turned the British right flank at Blackstocks where he was wounded, having to be carried from the field at Long Cane.

Clarke's most notable effort, however, came in carrying out the blockade of Augusta. In this endeavor he forced the notorious Tory Colonel, Thomas Browne, into near starvation until he, himself, was forced to retire by relief forces and leave behind thirty wounded men. Thirteen of the wounded were hanged by Browne; the others were tortured by Indians. The legendary Clarke continued to fight with brilliant hit-and-run guerrilla strategy, sweeping down on the British and then vanishing. Subsequently he had the satisfaction of being part of the forces which drove Browne from Augusta and one of the troops led by General Wayne in retaking Savannah. A grateful State of Georgia elevated his rank at the end of the war from

Colonel of the Continental Army to Major General of the Georgia Militia and conferred upon both him and John, who attained the rank of Major before his own majority, large grants of land.

A handsome and courtly man, though uncultured and unlettered, Clarke was chosen by Georgia to seek treaties with the Indians following the Revolution. His efforts, however, were thwarted largely due to the chicanery of half-breed Creek Chief Alexander McGillivray and the refusal of President Washington to make war on the Creeks. When the Indians invaded upper Georgia, Clarke and his son, Major John, marched against them, defeating them near Greensboro in the Battle of Jack's Creek, the name being in honor of a tribute to the son.

There followed, however, an episode which split father and son and brought the father to temporary disgrace. General Clarke, exhibiting his independent spirit and disdain for laws and orders with which he disagreed, accepted a commission as Major General in the French Army from Citizen Genet of the French Republic. He was to form and lead an army to wrest Louisiana from the Spanish. When that plan failed, Clarke marched his troops into Indian Territory to set up a Trans-Oconee Republic. The land, stretching ten miles wide and 120 miles down the length of the Oconee River, he proceeded to parcel out to his followers. On orders from President Washington to put an end to the venture, Georgia Governor George Mathews sent the Georgia Militia to destroy Clarke's settlements and to burn his three forts.

Scarred by the smallpox he contracted during the Revolution and still hurting from his old battle wounds, Clarke returned to his home where he died only a day after the death of his old commander and later nemesis, George Washington. An adoring public forgave Clarke, and his memory was honored by having a county, town, state park and dam and reservoir named for him. Ironically, his and Hannah's graves had to be relocated because of the waters of that reservoir.

John Clark, trading on his fame as a war hero and his rough, boyish charm, found a new niche in politics. He was destined to rise rapidly as the leader of the political faction of the Jefferson/Jackson Party composed largely of small farmers or "red-necks." They had been given this label by the opposing faction of wealthy planters led by William H. Crawford and George M. Troup.

Only slightly more literate than his father and burdened by a well-known propensity for indulgence in strong drink, John dropped the "e" from the spelling of the family name so no one would think him guilty of pretension or ostentation. He gathered around himself friends who supplied what he lacked in culture and who gave him unquestioned devotion. This would prove a pattern practiced in later years by Tom Watson and Gene Talmadge.

Clark was incensed when he was passed over for appointment as commander of Georgia troops in the War of 1812. Appointment by Governor Peter Early as a Major General of the Georgia Militia, the same rank held by his father, seemed to appease him. Drunken "sprees," numerous brawls, and challenges to duels with those who opposed him punctuated his daily life. He horsewhipped a brother-in-law whom he accused of cheating him. Twice he challenged the distinguished William H. Crawford to duels, a reflection of his ill feelings toward a man who was everything he was not. One of the duels was averted through the mediation of Governor John Milledge; the other was held in Indian Territory where Crawford was wounded painfully in the wrist. The factionalism which became personified in the personalities of Clark and Crawford's protege, Troup, continued for more than half a century. Perhaps its most, if not only, beneficial result was the direct election of governors by the people, a development which Clark engineered and which proved to be his political undoing.

At the height of Clark's power and popularity, governors were elected by the General Assembly. The body twice elected Clark as Chief Executive. But when his hand-picked successor was defeated by Troup himself, Clark launched a successful effort to amend the state constitution to provide for election of governors by the people. The first such popular election was held in 1825 with Clark personally opposing Troup for re-election. Troup was the victor by a margin of 682 votes. Ironically, a survey showed that a majority of the legislature would have elected Clark under the old system. This was the crowning indignity.

The ill-tempered Clark was so incensed at the turn of events that he sold all of his Georgia property and accepted an appointment from his friend, President Andrew Jackson, as Indian Agent in the Florida Territory. He bought several thousand acres of land on the West Coast of Florida overlooking St. Andrews Bay. In the luxurious home he built there for his family, he entertained many Georgia friends who traveled there to visit. But he was destined to die of yellow fever contracted on a trip across the Gulf of Mexico in his private sloop, a fate also suffered not long afterwards by his wife. Clark's property subsequently became the present City of St. Andrews. In 1921, under arrangements made by the Daughters of the American Revolution, his remains and those of his wife and two grandchildren were relocated from Florida to the Marietta National Cemetery. Efforts were made to locate any Clark descendants, but there was no response.

His biographer, George G. Smith, made this assessment:

"He might have had a far different fate had he possessed more self-restraint and been less the victim of his appetite for strong drink. . . . While more maligned, he was no worse a man than many of his associates; and of his general integrity, his sterling honesty, his devotion to his family, his unflinching courage, his open-handed generosity, and his loyalty to friends, there can be no question. He had great faults and great virtues."

Tyrus Raymond "Ty" Cobb

(Greatest Hitter in Baseball, First Member chosen for Baseball Hall of Fame. Philanthropist. Born December 18, 1886, Narrows, Banks County, Georgia. Died July 17, 1961, Cornelia, Georgia.

Until Hank Aaron came along in another generation to top some of their records, the fans of both Ty Cobb and Babe Ruth argued endlessly as to which of the two was the greatest baseball player of all time. But no one before or since has disputed the fact that "The Georgia Peach," the tag put on Cobb by sportswriter Grantland Rice, is the greatest and most consistent hitter the game has had since its invention by General Abner Doubleday in 1839. Cobb was also declared to be the most awesomely proficient, professionally respected, and personally feared man ever to don a baseball uniform.

The rage with which Cobb played the game is as legendary as his prowess in taking the measure of every pitcher he faced in twenty-four seasons of major league ball. "The Georgia Peach" was known to take on abusive fans with his fists, leaving basemen and catchers alike scarred by his slashing spikes. At the same time he posted a lifetime batting average of .367 which has since been exceeded by individual season averages of only Ted Williams and Stan Musial. While "The Hammer" topped Cobb in games played, times at bat, and total bases, his career batting average was only .305 and his hits were 420 less than Cobb's 5,863. When the Baseball Hall of Fame was opened in 1936, he received 222 of 226 votes to have the honor of being the first baseball great to be tapped for immortalization at Cooperstown.

Many self-appointed amateur psychologists have sought explanations for Cobb's angry, often cruel, and sometimes sadistic and masochistic behavior on and off the diamond. It was their conclusion these antics had their roots in the tragic

49

and bloody death of the father he loved so dearly. The elder Cobb died from a shotgun blast fired by his wife who mistook him for an intruder as he sought to entrap her in a suspected romantic liaison. Cobb's behavior also finds two other partial explanations. One was his obsession with the game of baseball which, with the possible exceptions of hunting and making money, was the only enduring interest of his life. The other was his monomaniacal determination to be first in everything he did. Brooklyn Pitcher Nap Rucker said that, when he and Cobb were roommates while rookies in the Sally League, Cobb even insisted on always being first to take a bath, explaining, "I've got to be first all of the time — first in everything."

Because baseball was his business, Cobb approached it as an art form to be mastered and controlled to the minutest detail. For him it was a game of brains as opposed to Ruth's game of brawn. Cobb always insisted that he made up for what he lacked in talent with determination and dedication. His mind was like a slide-rule, computing every aspect of the game from the effect of stance at the plate on pitchers to giving bases a couple of kicks to gain fractions of inches of advantage in stealing the next ones.

Cobb worked relentlessly. He practiced bunting by the hour to perfect the technique of dumping dead balls and sliding until his hips and thighs were raw. His aim was to develop the hook slide in which he caught the corners of bases with a toe and the faraway slide in which he avoided being tagged while reaching back to latch onto the bases with an outstretched arm. He hunted in heavy boots in the winter and wore lead weights in his shoes during spring training so he would feel light when running during the regular season. He even psyched the man he regarded as the game's greatest pitcher, Washington's Walter Johnson, into slowing his fast ball by crowding the plate, figuring correctly that the gentle Johnson would ease up rather than run the risk of shattering his ribs. But his greatest continuing feat was in intimidating basemen and catchers by sharpening his spikes and holding them high as he ran fast and hard to beat balls to the bags. The extra seconds he thus gained through the momentary defensive reflexes of his opponents added considerably to his record of 892 stolen bases.

Cobb's father wanted him to have a military or a legal career, but when he insisted on baseball he let him sign his first contract with Augusta in 1904 at the age of seventeen. When the Sally League team dropped him after he batted only .237 in thirty-seven games, the elder Cobb helped his son sign on with a semi-professional outfit in Anniston, but told him, "Don't come home a failure."

Cobb played as if possessed for the next twenty-four years, being brought back to Augusta after batting .370 in twenty-seven games in Alabama and then being sold to the Detroit Tigers for $750 the next year. In 1906 he signed a $1,500-a-year contract with the Tigers and had the first of twenty-three consecutive seasons in which he would bat .320 or better and three in which he would better the .400 mark. The following year he won the first of nine consecutive batting championships and played in the first of three consecutive World Series, all of which Detroit lost. Ironically, these were the only World Championships in which Cobb ever had the opportunity to play.

In 1911 he broke .400, posting .420 for the season and winning his only Most Valuable Player Award. In 1912 he engaged in a bitter contract holdout until May 1, finally signing for a salary of $11,332.55. That was the beginning of the yearly escalations in pay until, at the height of his career, he was receiving a record $50,000 a year. This money he wisely invested in Coca-Cola and General Motors stock which made him a fortune reputed to be in excess of $12-million at the time of his death.

In 1915, he set a record of stealing ninety-six bases, a record which stood until topped by Maury Wills of the Los Angeles Dodgers in 1962. Cobb dropped the batting title in 1916, but regained it for the next three years. When Detroit slipped to seventh place in 1920, he was appointed manager in 1921, the year Ruth came to the Yankees. Under Cobb's direction the team finished sixth that year, third in 1922, second in 1923, third in 1924, and sixth in 1926.

He and Cleveland Player-Manager Tris Speaker were fired in 1926 after American League President Ban Johnson accused them of "fixing" a game between the two teams for betting purposes in 1919. Although cleared by Commissioner Kenesaw Mountain Landis and restored to the Detroit Roster, he was released and signed by Connie Mack to play two seasons for the Philadelphia Athletics. There he batted .357 in 1927, retiring the following year after dropping to .323. He was forty-one.

Cobb's escapades and tantrums were well publicized during his career. He was suspended for going into the stands in New York and thrashing a fan who called him an obscene name. He was sued by a New York hotel chambermaid who accused him

51

of beating her after she expressed resentment about him calling her a "nigger." He called Hornus Wagner "a kraut" and threatened to spike him on the basepaths in the 1909 World Series. He fought under the stands with American League Umpire Billy Evans. He brawled in a hotel room with New York giant Buck Herzog. He almost got himself beaten into a bloody pulp by Detroit Catcher Germany Schmidt, a powerful man fifty pounds heavier than Cobb, whom he insisted upon fighting despite Schmidt's efforts to turn away.

While Cobb always denied accusations that he deliberately tried to spike Home Run Baker in 1909, he not only gave Yankee Catcher Bootnose Hofmann his scars intentionally but told him in advance what he was going to do after Hofmann belittled his "Georgia Peach" handle. Using his spikes as he slid into home, he tore off Hofmann's chest protector and shinguard and ripped his thigh. His conduct made him so unpopular with his teammates that they often would not speak to him. Frequently he dined alone. Writers agreed he was one of the most disliked players in baseball history. His personal life was equally stormy. He was divorced twice and was not close to the two of his five children who outlived him.

Cobb mellowed somewhat in his later years and used his fortune to build and equip a hospital named in honor of his father in Royston. He also established an educational foundation to provide scholarships to deserving college students who had proved themselves by getting through their freshman years without assistance. His retirement years were divided between Georgia and Lake Tahoe, Nevada. At the time of his death from cancer and other disabilities, he was in Cornelia, Georgia, talking about building a home on Chenocetah Mountain.

On his last visit to Cooperstown, Cobb freely discussed with friends the color and controversy of his career. Of his reputation he asserted, "I wasn't nearly as rough as everyone said."

William Harris Crawford

(Lawyer, United States Senator, Minister to France, Secretary of War, Secretary of the Treasury, Judge. Born February 24, 1772, Nelson County, Virginia. Died September 15, 1834, Elberton, Georgia.)

In another day and time William Harris Crawford could have become a matinee idol. Certainly he had the looks to be one and the adjectives handsome and dashing seem to have been coined to describe his striking appearance. Blond, blue-eyed, ruddy, muscular, and standing six feet three inches tall, the sight of him prompted the Emperor Napoleon to remark that he was the only man to whom he ever felt inclined to bow.

But there was more to him than good looks, both positive and negative. A biographer commented that "his jaw and chin showed firmness of character . . . and upon looking at him one felt that here was a man who possessed extraordinary intellectual power." In assessing Crawford's strengths and weaknesses the revered Albert Gallatin, whom he succeeded as Secretary of the Treasury, wrote: "he united to a powerful mind a most correct judgment and an inflexible integrity; which last quality, not sufficiently tempered by indulgence and civility, has prevented his acquiring general popularity."

In short, Crawford had a hot temper and little time for suffering fools, traits which got him into a lot of verbal and physical violence. He was a participant in two duels. In one he killed a man, and in the other he himself was wounded. Another confrontation involved President James Monroe shortly after the two of them had drafted the Monroe Doctrine at Crawford's Georgia home. The President ordered Crawford out of the White House after the two of them had threatened each other, one with a walking cane and the other with a fire poker.

Coming to Georgia from Virginia as a nine-year-old and finding it necessary to drop out of school to help his mother support the family after the death of his father from smallpox, Crawford's education was mostly self-acquired. He did, however, spend some time in the famous school of Moses Waddell also attended by Waddell's brother-in-law, John C. Calhoun. It was here the enmity which would characterize the later relations between Crawford and Calhoun, when both came into national prominence, was born.

Crawford's legal learning, also self-taught, made him sufficiently prosperous to attract the hand in marriage of Susannah Giradin, the beautiful daughter of a French Huguenot plantation owner. With her he built his beloved home, Woodlawn, near Lexington in Oglethorpe County. He also got himself elected to the Georgia Legislature where he quickly became the upland ally of James Jackson and George M. Troup. This political faction generally favored wealthy, slave-owning planters as opposed to that of John Clark who championed the causes of the poor red-neck farmers who had to scratch their own livings out of the soil. Crawford, being in the right place at the right time, was named to succeed the late Abraham Baldwin whose death created a vacancy in the United States Senate. Because of the volatile nature of Georgia's peculiar brand of personality politics, Crawford found himself caught up in two duels. In one he killed Clark's protege, State Attorney General Peter Van Allen, and in the other, Clark wounded Crawford in the wrist, making the two of them bitter enemies for life.

Crawford worked hard at establishing himself as a respected and effective legislator. He had a quick mind and an ability to absorb and master complicated subjects swiftly and thoroughly. Although he was not an eloquent orator, his ready wit, his capacity for grasping and articulating subtle nuances, and his ability to call on a stock of appropriate stories recounted with inimitable style rapidly elevated him to leadership and influence in the Upper Chamber. As a result, in 1812 he was elected President Pro Tempore of this body, upon the death of Vice President George Clinton. It was, however, on the subject of the renewal of the charter of the Bank of the United States that he put himself on the path that led to the doorsteps of the White House. Except for the failure of his health, Crawford instead of John Quincy Adams would have been the next President.

Whether it was out of personal opportunism in the furthering of his own political fortunes or out of brilliant perception of the future fiscal requirements of the nation (and it has been argued both ways), Crawford broke with his fellow followers of Thomas Jefferson. He waged a campaign for the granting of a new charter to the Bank of the United States upon the expiration of its original 20-year grant of authority in 1811. With behind-the-scenes help and advice from Treasury Secretary Gallatin, Crawford led the fight for the bank. The great Henry Clay of Kentucky was the principal spokesman for the opponents.

The resulting debate was one of the most profound and intense in Senate history, either before or since. Crawford's audacity in challenging the perfection of the Constitution, which to that point had been treated as second only in sanctity to the Holy Scriptures, was sensational. Equally shocking was his challenge to duel a Tennessee Senator who accused him of apostasy if the remark were repeated outside the Chamber. Because of his effective strategy and his persuasive debating, Crawford brought what was a foregone defeat for the bank to a tie vote, a tie broken (against the bank) only by the vote of the Vice President. Defeat was by a similar one-vote margin in the House of Representatives. And, although the greatest effort of his senatorial career ended in failure, he had the satisfaction five years later of seeing those who had opposed him have to reverse themselves and vote to give the bank another 20-year charter.

Crawford's national stature grew rapidly thereafter. In quick succession President James Madison named him Minister to France, Secretary of War, and, on the recommendation of Former Secretary Gallatin, Secretary of the Treasury. He continued in the latter position throughout the eight years of the term of President James Monroe against whom he declined to be a candidate for the presidency in 1816. Crawford exercised tremendous influence over President Monroe and his administration and generally is credited with the idea and much of the substance of the Monroe Doctrine. He was the leading contender to succeed Monroe and undoubtedly would have been elected but for the onslaught of a mysterious, paralyzing illness which temporarily crippled him and left him virtually deaf and blind. For these reasons, his supporters deserted him. The election was thrown into the House of Representatives where Andrew Jackson, who had polled the most votes, was defeated by John Quincy Adams. Adams offered Crawford a post in his Cabinet but ill health caused him to decline.

Crawford returned to Georgia a sick and broken old man. At

his beloved Woodlawn, his neighbors, shocked by his frailty, treated him with all the deference due a returning hero. He slowly regained his strength to the point where, upon the death of Judge John Dooly, Governor Peter Early appointed him to the circuit judgeship. He served in this position from 1827 until his death on September 15, 1834. Death came while Crawford was visiting his new grandchild in what is now Elbert County. He was buried in the shade of a magnolia tree near Woodlawn. The house subsequently burned and his lone tomb stands as a seldom-visited and virtually-forgotten monument to the great and handsome Georgian who almost was President.

His epitaph tells his story:

"Sacred to the memory of William Harris Crawford, born 24th February 1772 in Nelson County, Va. Died 15th September 1834, in Oglethorpe County, Georgia. In the Legislature of Georgia, as Minister to the Court of France, in the Cabinet, and on the Bench, he was alike independent, energetic, fearless, and able. He died as he lived, in the service of his country and left behind him the unimpeachable fame of an honest name."

The cherished cherry tree given him by Napoleon — planted outside his bedroom window at Woodlawn where he could view it from his sickbed — has long since perished. But the uniform he wore when he made his indelible impression upon his presentation to the French Emperor is a prized exhibit in the Georgia Department of Archives and History in Atlanta.

William Lamar Dodd

 *(Artist, Educator, Lecturer, Official Artist for National Aeronautics and Space Administration. Born September 22, 1909, Fairburn, Georgia. Resides Athens, Georgia.)*

Dr. William Lamar Dodd has received in life the recognition and acclaim that few artists achieve before their deaths. While critics may disagree in categorizing the style and significance of his techniques and subjects, there is a consensus that he is one of the greatest artists of the Twentieth Century, if not the greatest. This recognition is worldwide, because his works are as well known behind the Iron Curtain as in the Free World.

Testimony to his stature is the fact that he is one of very few artists of any period to have a major gallery specifically designed and constructed to house and display his paintings and drawings. The Lamar Dodd Art Center built on the campus of LaGrange College by the Callaway Foundation not only will showcase his works and teach aspiring future artists but also will insure that his rank in the history of art will be enhanced and perpetuated for all time.

Lamar Dodd is an unlikely artist from any standpoint because he fits none of the stereotypes of the genre. One would not have expected his background and development to have produced such a man. Nor does he even look or act like an artist. In fact, if he appeared on "What's My Line?" his silver hair, handsome features, retiring demeanor, and ever-present pipe would cause panelists to speculate on his profession. Some would label him a kindly grandfather who probably was a judge, a United States Senator, or a character actor in the movies. Certainly no one would guess that he is the product of the New York City of the Depression where "Bohemian" was the mildest of adjectives applied to the artists of that era or that he has evolved to be a space age artist in the most literal sense of the term.

It probably would be more nearly correct to call him "the" space age artist because he was named Official Artist for the National Aeronautics and Space Administration. His canvases reflect the asthetics as well as the technology of the Mercury, Gemini, Apollo, and Space Shuttle space explorations, and have attracted virtually unanimous critical acclaim.

His unique capacity for communicating emotion through structure and color — which had caused some of his earlier and more mundane presentations to be dismissed as "regional" —proved the perfect technique for giving visual embodiment to the spiritual meaning of space exploration as he saw it. This quality elevated his work above the science fiction, gadgetry, and photograpic illustration techniques of fellow artists tackling the same subject matter.

Edmund Burke Feldman described his drawings of the space vehicle launchings as "a powerful impression of intelligently contained and directed energy." Dodd's renderings of the space capsule in flight "seem to divest that infinite realm of any aura of hostility to man and his works," Feldman said. W. C. Burnett, Jr., arts editor of **The Atlanta Journal,** commented that Dodd's use of blacks, golds, and light grays "suggested vistas of space," describing his textural effects as "almost sculptural." It is not surprising that Dodd now has moved on to apply the same approach and technique to open heart surgery. This interest was inspired by his beloved wife Mary's recent surgery, prompting a vow that he would go on painting in this new field "for the rest of my life."

Dodd grew up in the strict but stimulating environment of a Baptist preacher's home. He attributes the Calvinist conscience and perfectionism which underlie his approaches to depicting the subjects of his canvases to that upbringing. The artist was a precocious youngster who raised rabbits, guinea pigs, pigeons, and chickens. His Rhode Island Reds and Bantams won a number of prizes at county fairs. But his greatest fun as a youth was in riding his pony and helping his uncle who owned a livery stable herd mules from the railroad station to the stable.

Things changed for him, however, when he won a prize in a sixth grade art contest. With a watercolor of sailboats which he learned to copy to perfection. Young Dodd began demonstrating such promise that his mother, herself a lady of artistic interests and abilities, obtained special permission to enroll him in an art class at LaGrange College at the age of twelve. Although LaGrange was a Methodist girl's school, he was

58

allowed to study there after it was determined he was not a threat to the virtue of his distaff classmates. An extant photograph of the class shows a serious and obviously uncomfortable young Dodd working at his easel in the midst of a sea of female compatriots similarly occupied. He soon advanced from copying to drawing and painting. When he was graduated from high school, he was presented a special certificate from LaGrange College along with his diploma.

He then started studying architecture at Georgia Institute of Technology but dropped out after doing more drawing and sketching than drafting. At Tech he did absorb certain architectural techniques which characterize his style and continue to influence his work. Notable among these are his use of the right angle and his tendency to express feeling through structure.

Dodd taught high school art for a year in Alabama before his move to New York City for further study. Encouraged by a banker friend who told him "a man has to have the guts to do what he has to do," Dodd went to the metropolis where he studied for two years with George Bridgeman and Boardman Robinson at the Art Students League. In addition, he had private instruction from George Luks and Charles Martin. In this setting he became grounded in the philosophy of the "Ash Can School" in which artists draw from objects in the everyday world instead of from literary or classical themes.

He returned to LaGrange in 1930 to marry his one and only sweetheart, Mary Ridley Lehman. For the next year he drew the rural scenes, faces, and themes which have so influenced his later works. And in 1931 he held his first exhibit, at the High Museum of Art in Atlanta.

Despite the Depression, the Dodds traveled to New York where they both worked and painted. He studied with John Stewart Curry and John Charlot, a protege of Diego Riviera. Dodd later would attract Charlot to the University of Georgia as an artist in residence. Economic necessity eventually forced the couple to Birmingham, Alabama, where for three years he managed an art supply store by day and painted by night. After a stint as guest artist at Colorado Springs Fine Arts Center, Dodd received an invitation to join the faculty of the University of Georgia. There he attracted the admiration of the great Georgia pianist Hugh Hodgson who, when asked to establish a Fine Arts Department at the University, persuaded President Harmon W. Caldwell to make Dodd head of the Art Department despite his lack of an academic degree. Hodgson liked to tell the story that he convinced Dr. Caldwell to make the appointment by telling him of overhearing two professors discussing one of his recitals and speculating on whether artistic performance really required intellectual capabilities.

At the University of Georgia Dodd developed the Art Department from two and one-half to fifty-five faculty members over the course of his tenure which lasted until retirement in 1974. Four years earlier he had been named by the Board of Regents of the University System of Georgia the first appointee to the Lamar Dodd Professional Chair of Art which it established in his honor. This position he still holds in emeritus status.

During his years on the Athens campus, Dodd produced thousands of practicing artists, teachers, and curators who spread his fame throughout the world. More importantly, as the result of his efforts over the past forty years, Georgia was transformed from a state in which there were no institutions offering professional art education to one in which a number of Georgia universities and colleges offer quality as well as diverse art instruction. No aspiring young Georgia artists need now go elsewhere for their education.

After Dodd entered the academic world, degrees and honors were not long in coming, including a Doctor of Humane Letters bestowed on him by LaGrange College. He was also the recipient of a long succession of prizes, awards, and grants, and his work was widely sought.

The Metropolitan Museum of Art acquired his famous canvas "Sand Sea and Sky" in 1940 and added "Monhegan Theme" in 1951. Other major paintings also were acquired by the Whitney Museum of American Art, the Pennsylvania Academy of the Fine Arts, the Air and Space Museum of the Smithsonian Institute, the High Museum of Art, and other notable galleries.

Dodd was named one of the thirteen outstanding American artists in 1939, with paintings being purchased by International Business Machines, Pepsi-Cola, and other major firms. He also received a Rockefeller Foundation grant for study abroad. Since 1930, he has held more than 100 major one-man exhibitions throughout the world. In addition, he lectured in a number of European universities, was elected a Fellow in the Royal Society of Arts of London, and traveled to Russia and the Far East as Special Representative of the U. S. State Department.

Other honors included election to Phi Beta Kappa. He also served two terms as President of the College Art Association of

America and in various capacities with other national, regional, and state arts organizations. Three agencies of the U. S. Government named him their Official Artist — NASA, the Environmental Protection Agency, and the Bureau of Reclamation of the Department of the Interior.

Lamar and Mary Dodd donated a collection of 200 of his paintings and drawings to LaGrange College and will leave a similar selection of his works to the University of Georgia. Both collections are fully representative of what he has done throughout the spectrum of his career.

Two things that definitely can be said about Dodd's work are: it has character and provokes strong feelings. Young artists dedicated to experimental approaches have found his style reactionary and some have dismissed his paintings as parochial. While it is true he has eschewed the more esoteric forms, he employed aspects of analytical cubism before it became avant garde in the 50's and, while never discarding nature as his major inspiration, he moved into symbolism in the late 60's and 70's.

Feldman describes Dodd's ruling technique as an amalgam of the emotionalism, mysticism, excitement, and senuousness of El Greco restrained and contained by the defined structure of Cezanne. Whatever the specific influences, Dodd himself regards his painting as a form of communication which emphasizes relationships and seeks to create self-contained completeness in each presentation. In other words, he paints to convey feelings and to give meaning to those feelings.

Dodd himself sums up Dodd and his work in this way: "Painting is the product of man, his urge to share with others his feelings and impulses. Regardless of the form it may take, it is and always has been a form of communication. If a painting is to have meaning to mankind, if it is to survive through the ages, it must have certain inherent qualities that are timeless, regardless of the place or time it was created."

Rebecca Ann Latimer Felton

(Columnist, Author, Reformer, Feminist Crusader, Political Leader, Congressional Secretary, First Female United States Senator. Born June 10, 1835, DeKalb County, Georgia. Died January 24, 1930, Atlanta, Georgia.)

No one believed Grandma Felton ever would sit in the United States Senate. Everything was against her, including the Senate precedent set in 1815 that no appointed Senator would be seated after a successor was elected. Even her friend, President Warren G. Harding, who had appointed her to his Presidential Advisory Commission, refused to call a Special Session of Congress to swear her in.

But the pundits and the parliamentarians reckoned without the grit and determination of the redoubtable, 87-year-old Georgia crusader. Dressed in black dress and bonnet, she created quite a sensation when she presented herself in the previously all-male sanctorum and defied her "colleagues" to deny her right to take the oath as the first female United States Senator. This was a drama which captivated even blasé Washington. Thus Rebecca Ann Latimer Felton climaxed her long, colorful, and controversial career as a political mover-and-shaker by toppling the walls of male chauvinism in the World's Greatest Deliberative Body on November 21, 1922. The action came only a little more than two years after the ratification of the 19th Amendment which gave women the right to vote, a cause in which she also was active.

Two events set the stage for this historic event. One was the death of Mrs. Felton's political idol, fire-eating Senator Thomas E. Watson. The second was her appointment as a "seat-warmer" by another political compatriot, Governor Thomas W. Hardwick, who unsuccessfully sought the seat. All of this occurred while Congress was in adjournment.

Women's organizations throughout the country crusaded unsuccessfully for a special session of Congress so Mrs. Felton could be a legislative pioneer for her sex. The day was saved by the courtesy of the courtly Senator-elect, Walter Franklin George. George withheld his credentials of election for one day to permit Mrs. Felton, the appointee of the governor he had defeated, to be sworn in. Following a brief, witty address to the Senate, Rebecca Felton returned to her home in Cartersville. So formidable was her appearance and so popular her cause that no senator dared rise to oppose her. As for George, it was the first of many acts of statesmanship which were to make him one of the greatest senators of all time.

Rebecca was a precocious child who excelled in music, languages, composition, and literature. She particularly enjoyed listening to her father, the postmaster of Decatur, read letters and newspapers to illiterate patrons. As a teenager she was a charmer and, as co-first-honor graduate of Madison Female College, she so captivated Dr. William Harrell Felton, the parson-physician who was the commencement speaker and twelve years her senior, that they were married before her eighteenth birthday.

From this union, which has been described as a lifelong love affair, came five children, all but one of whom died before maturity. The Feltons were inseparable in everything from running their farm, establishing and operating their school, publishing their newspaper, to sharing a refugee shack in Macon. When Sherman invaded Georgia, the couple fled to Bibb County where Dr. Felton served as a physician to Confederate troops.

Rebecca was Dr. Felton's secretary during the three terms he served in Congress. In the nation's capital she became a prominent figure known to the greats and near-greats spanning half a century. She was often criticized severely for her forward political actions, like appearing at rallies and writing strong letters to the editors of newspapers. **The Thomasville Times** once took her to task editorially when it wrote, "We sincerely trust that the example set by Mrs. Felton will not be followed by Southern Ladies." Her husband often was ridiculed because of her aggressiveness, an example being the jingle used against him in one of his campaigns:

"Some parsons hide behind their coat
To save their precious life;
But Parson Felton beats them all,
He hides behind his wife."

While serving in the state legislature, Dr. Felton took exception to the reference to him as "the great political she of Georgia" with an outburst of denunciation described as "one of the very worst excoriations known to Chaucer's English."

The Feltons became political activists in the wake of the economic hardships suffered by themselves and other poor and lower middle-class North Georgia farmers following the Civil War. Particularly was this the result of the policies of the Bourbon Democrats led by Joseph E. Brown, Alfred H. Colquitt, and John B. Gordon which pursued the interests of the former planter aristocracy and the new business entrepreneurs. Because he filled many pulpits over a wide area of Northwest Georgia, Dr. Felton became a symbol and spokesman for the Independent Movement, resulting in his election to three terms in Congress, beginning in 1874, as representative from the Seventh District.

With the help of his wife's pen and labors, Dr. Felton compiled a distinguished record in Congress on two matters in particular: his opposition to monopolies and in taking positions which were forerunners of those of the Populists two decades later. The Independent threat so frightened the Bourbons that they counterattacked with charges that the Feltons were allied with the Republicans and were a threat to white supremacy. He was unseated in 1880. The Independents countered with an attempt to nominate former Vice President of the Confederacy Alexander Hamilton Stephens for Governor in 1882. But that, too, was thwarted by the Bourbons who offered Stephens their nomination and a sure electoral victory.

In 1890 and 1894, Dr. Felton again unsuccessfully sought election to Congress. After his defeat in 1880, most of the time and effort of both his wife and himself were devoted to state politics. Here they enjoyed greater success. As a member of the General Assembly, Dr. Felton successfully opposed sale of the state-owned Western and Atlantic Railroad to a company headed by Joseph E. Brown and the enactment of legislation gutting the Georgia Railroad Commission.

Through their newspaper, **The Cartersville Courant,** Mrs. Felton kept up a steady drumbeat of editorial opposition to the schemes and programs of the Brown-Colquitt-Gordon "Bourbon Triumvirate." She was also noted for carrying on the greatest and longest crusade of their careers against the infamous convict lease system in which companies of both Brown and Gordon were major participants.

She persistently and meticulously documented the abuses

in which men, women, and children were forced into common prisons where they were systemically subjected to near starvation and inhumane conditions. The establishment of a juvenile reformatory was one of her pet projects. While Dr. Felton's legislation on the subject was not enacted, she lived long enough to see the lease system abolished by law and separate facilities established for men, women, and juvenile offenders.

In 1889, Hoke Smith, publisher of **The Atlanta Journal,** employed Mrs. Felton to write a column for his paper. This she continued to do until her death in 1930. On the strength of the column, she achieved a statewide constituency which had great respect for her opinions. She commented on every President from Cleveland to Harding, particularly favoring Theodore Roosevelt and opposing Woodrow Wilson. Her favorite political personality, however, was Thomas E. Watson, leader of the Progressive Party in Georgia.

She was a leader in the Woman's Christian Temperance Union and was a successful crusader for prohibition in Georgia. She opposed American entry into World War I and membership in the League of Nations. She took an active role in the gubernatorial campaign of the man who appointed her to the Senate, and her writings evoked the attack from Clifford Walker charging that Hardwick was a Communist and Mrs. Felton and William Randolph Hearst, publisher of **The Atlanta Georgian,** were involved "in the Russian conspiracy." One of the Walker leaders later commented that "we stepped right into the middle of hell itself when we stirred up that Mrs. Felton."

It was fitting that Mrs. Felton delivered the eulogy at memorial services for Watson and then succeeded him in the Senate.

During the course of her long life and career, Mrs. Felton wrote literally millions of words in columns, letters to the editor, and her three books: **My Memoirs of Georgia Politics** (1911), **Country Life in Georgia in the Days of My Youth** (1919), and **The Romantic Story of Georgia's Women** (1930).

Her biographer, Josephine Bone Floyd, summed up her almost ninety-five years of life and more than six decades in the mainstream of state and national events thusly: "She was a constructive force in the political life of Georgia. This was seen in her fight against the sale of the Western and Atlantic and in giving publicity to the attack on the Georgia Railroad Commission. She made a decided liberal contribution to the

State in arousing public opinion to the evils of the convict lease system and in fighting for the establishment of a juvenile reformatory. Her voice, although not always consistent, was a powerful one in Georgia politics particularly from the World War to her death in 1930, and she expressed her opinions with complete fearlessness. And in most cases it can be truthfully said that she had the welfare of the common people at heart."

William Few

(Lawyer, Banker, Revolutionary Soldier, Member of Continental Congress, Signer of United States Constitution, United States Senator, Judge, Member of Georgia and New York General Assemblies. Born June 8, 1748, near Baltimore, Maryland. Died July 16, 1828, Fishkill, New York. Reinterred Under Monument in Downtown Augusta, Georgia.)

It took almost a century and a half, a Bicentennial Celebration, the joint efforts of Governors Jimmy Carter of Georgia and Nelson Rockefeller of New York, and judicial proceedings lasting longer than a year to locate his descendants for the State of Georgia to give William Few the honor in death whose denial in life caused him to leave the state with the vow never to return.

But thanks to the tenacity of Clifford M. Clarke, Jr., Vice Chairman of the Georgia Commission for the National Bicentennial Celebration, and the approval and assistance of Milo B. Howard, Jr., Director of the Alabama Department of Archives and History and Few's great-great-great-great-nephew, the bones of William Few were returned to Georgia from a desecrated tomb in New York and given a place of perpetual honor under a granite monument to his memory on the lawn of a church in his former hometown of Augusta.

A native of Maryland who was educated in North Carolina, Few came to Georgia at the age of twenty-eight and made quite a name for himself in twenty years of military and public service. Eventually he quit in anger after the Georgia Legislature denied him a second term in the United States Senate. During the course of those two decades he had served as a Lieutenant Colonel in the Richmond County Militia during the

American Revolution, as a Member of the Georgia House of Representatives, as a Delegate to the Continental Congress, and as a Delegate to the Constitutional Convention. He was one of two Georgians to sign the Constitution of the United States, was one of Georgia's first two United States Senators, was an original Trustee of the University of Georgia, and was a Circuit Court Judge.

According to the notes of William Pierce, a delegate who was not present for the signing of the Constitution, Few was a "strong natural Genius" who participated faithfully in the deliberations but never spoke a word in the debates. In his memoirs, the modest Few did not even mention the fact that he was one of Georgia's two signers of the document.

In recognition of his service, the Georgia General Assembly elected him to the "short term" as one of the state's first two senators in 1789, establishing the succession to that seat now held by Sam Nunn as the "Few Line," but he did not offer for reelection when it ended in 1793. He apparently had a change of heart, however, for when a vacancy occurred two years later, he offered as a candidate and was incensed when he was not chosen to again occupy the seat. After completing his term as a Circuit Court Judge, he moved with his family to New York, writing later in his memoirs of his humiliation:

"It was one of the greatest mortifications I had ever experienced; it was indeed the first of the kind I had met with. Notwithstanding, I now believe it to be one of the most fortunate events of my life, for if I had obtained that appointment, I should have most probably spent the remainder of my days in the scorching climate of Georgia, under all the accumulating evils of fevers and Negro slavery, those enemies of humane felicity."

Few had a second career in both public service and banking in New York. He served as an Alderman in Fishkill (now Beacon) and a member of the New York State Assembly and became a wealthy man as president of the Manhattan Bank. He also served as State Prison Inspector and as United States Commissioner of Loans. He died at the age of eighty in Fishkill at the home of his son-in-law, Major Albert Chrystie. The Federal-style mansion where Few died has been restored as a showplace by its present owner, a physician. He was interred in the Chrystie family mausoleum in the cemetery of the Reformed Dutch Church of Fishkill. The mausoleum fell into disrepair and was abandoned and vandalized after the turn of the century. It was from that tomb that his remains were recovered and returned to Georgia.

Georgia made its first effort to pay belated honor to Few in 1939 when his "lost" burial place was identified by opening the vault and finding with the bones the silver casket nameplate, "William Few, died the 16th day of July A.D. 1828 in the 80th year of his age." The tomb was resealed and a marble marker placed at its entrance by the Georgia Sons of the American Revolution.

A second brief and abortive attempt to return Few's remains to Georgia came in 1966 during the administration of Governor Carl Sanders. It was abandoned, however, because the Sons and Daughters of the American Revolution could not agree on who should do what.

Nothing further was done until J. Moreau Brown, III, a New York attorney active in the Sons of the American Revolution, told Clarke at a meeting of the National Bicentennial Commission of the collapse of the mausoleum roof and the desecration of the grave. It was Brown's strong recommendation that Georgia renew its efforts. Clarke obtained the approval of Governor Carter, and recovery of the Georgia hero's remains was made a major project of the Bicentennial Celebration.

Opposition to the removal developed within the Reformed Church and, despite the fact that it had abandoned the cemetery, its Consistory questioned whether Few or his descendants would wish for his remains to be returned to the state he left in a huff. There was a contention that Few, in his last will and testament, had imposed a prohibition against such later reinterment, but research proved that not to be the case.

At the insistence of the Church, legal proceedings for authorization of the removal were instituted in the Supreme Court of Duchess County where the judge required a family tree and approval of all living descendants. Although many Fews were found, only one living direct descendant was discovered, a 17-year-old Indianian named Dennie Michael Russak who had never even heard of his illustrious ancestor. Accordingly, Clarke prevailed upon Howard, as the nearest living relative interested in the matter, to sign the petition to the Court. Clarke also requested Governor Carter to seek the assistance of Governor Rockefeller while both were attending the 1972 National Governors Conference in Texas. Governor Rockefeller was sympathetic, saying, "I'll get him back to Georgia if I have to dig him up myself." His staff proceeded to cut red tape and to expedite the judicial proceedings. As a result, Judge Joseph F. Hawkins signed an order of removal on December 4, 1972, stating that Georgia's plans for a monument and burial site in Augusta were "far more befitting Few's role in American history."

On January 29, 1973, Dr. Lewis Larson, State Archaeologist, and Dr. Larry Howard, Director of the State Crime Laboratory, separated bones from the beer cans and other debris in the tomb. They were able to identify, among other things, an intact lower jawbone with the full set of teeth the 80-year-old Few was said to have possessed when he died. The remains were placed in a child's bronze casket, covered by an American Flag, and flown by Clarke back to Georgia in the Governor's plane. They were reinterred in Augusta under a large monument provided by the Elberton Granite Association. The inscription included all Few's achievements. Enroute the plane made a brief stop at Washington, D. C., to discharge a passenger, thus also giving Few his first visit to the nation's current capital, it having been New York at the time of his service in the Senate.

Milo Howard said he felt his great-great-great-great-uncle, a Quaker who was opposed to slavery, would have approved of being returned to Georgia with the honors he once was denied. Howard felt his ancestor would have approved of what had been done in the intervening years to "wipe out the last vestiges of that evil legacy." He posed for a photograph with Few's bust in the rotunda of the Georgia Capitol and expressed the belief that his distinguished forebear also would have liked the inscription it bore: "His course in the National Councils was marked by integrity, fidelity and ability."

Walter Franklin George

(Lawyer, Judge, United States Senator, President Pro Tempore of the United States Senate, Diplomat. Born January 19, 1878, near Preston, Georgia. Died January 4, 1957, Vienna, Georgia.)

Walter Franklin George was a rare politician who could be described as a true statesman. He did not slap backs, kiss babies, or engage in demagoguery to win votes, yet he never lost an election. He spoke only when he had something to say, but he was a powerful orator who could hold and move an audience like a virtuoso playing a mighty pipe organ. He legislated quietly without fanfare or publicity, but he is acknowledged to have been without peer before or since in shaping and influencing legislation during his thirty-four years in the United States Senate. He was denounced at one time or another by both liberals and conservatives, but he never was swayed from following principle as he saw it or voting for what he believed to be right.

Born into the poverty of a post-Civil War tenant farm family in Southwest Georgia, young Walter early established himself as one from whom much was expected because his favorite childhood pastime was reading and memorizing speeches from **The Congressional Record.** His course to greatness was set the day he rode a bareback mule into Preston at the age of sixteen to attend Confederate Memorial Day ceremonies at which he wound up being invited to substitute for the speaker who did not show up. He won great acclaim with a 40-minute extemporaneous address on "The Duties of a Citizen" patterned on a Congressional oration about Robert E. Lee he had committed to memory.

He paid his way through the Law School later to bear his name at Mercer University, by teaching grade school. There he spurned athletics for debate and declamation and was graduated with membership in Phi Beta Kappa. Returning to Southwest Georgia, he borrowed $300 and bought out the equally-skimpy library and practice of a lawyer in Vienna who wanted to go west to prospect for oil. Through assiduous preparation, the young lawyer won every case in his first term of court. The other lawyers in town eagerly backed him when he offered his candidacy for Solicitor-General of the Cordele Circuit Court in 1907, a post he held until appointed to the Circuit Judgeship in 1910.

While Judge, George attracted statewide attention by using his eloquence to dissuade a mob bent upon lynching a white man accused of killing a county official. In 1916, he was elected to the Georgia Court of Appeals from which he was appointed to the Georgia Supreme Court the following year. He served as Associate Justice until he resigned in 1922 to return home to handle the estate of Joseph Heard, the father of his wife whom he called "Miss Lucy." While fishing with a friend on the Flint River later that year, he heard of the death of colorful Senator Thomas E. Watson and decided to run for his unexpired term.

His election over a field of seven candidates astounded everyone. In the race he received the unsolicited support of the Ku Klux Klan whose members got even with his principal opponent, Governor Thomas Hardwick, for his crusade to unmask that secret organization. And most Georgians, thinking back on the tumultuous career of his predecessor Watson, figured they had heard the last of the aloof and unspectacular George.

But George managed to achieve attention immediately by deferring the presentation of his credentials of election for one day so that Senator Watson's appointed interim successor, the women's suffrage crusader Mrs. Rebecca Latimer Felton, might be sworn in as the first female member of the United States Senate.

With characteristic thoroughness and diligent study George became the Senate's foremost expert on tariffs and taxation in his early years, a process later repeated in the field of foreign policy. Over the course of his Senate career, he served on twelve different committees and was chairman of five. One of these was the tax-writing Finance Committee during World War II and the Korean War. Twice during crucial periods that followed he chaired the Foreign Relations Committee where he sponsored the Eisenhower Formosa Resolution and succeeded in his call for a Big Four meeting in 1955 to discuss means of averting a third world war.

72

The Senator's mellowing over the years from an opponent of the League of Nations to an ardent and vocal advocate of world peace had its genesis in the loss of his flier son, Marcus, over the Atlantic during World War II. One of his last statements on the subject was, "America should be big enough to talk to anyone in the interest of world peace," and his support of foreign aid handed his successor the issue which led to his retirement.

George was a champion of free enterprise. Often he was accused by his detractors of serving "big interests" in his viewpoints, but his record does not bear that out. To the contrary, he consistently favored economy in government, tax reductions for average people, and progressive measures benefitting the masses. He was a staunch supporter of vocational education, and his proudest accomplishment was authoring every major piece of legislation on the subject from 1929 through 1946. He was a dogged advocate of a veterans' bonus, twice voting to override presidential vetoes of such legislation.

For all of his dignity and patrician reserve, he lived simply, cherished his privacy, and detested and avoided Washington functions. Although he was a fastidious dresser who favored crisp double-breasted white suits, immaculate white shirts, and panama hats, he so abhorred formal dress that Presidents would change occasions to informal to insure his attendance. He used his formal wear so seldom that Miss Lucy once made over his swallowtail coat into a suit for herself. He did not miss it until he needed it to wear to a reception for the Queen of the Netherlands.

He considered himself a "born Democrat," received 58½ votes for President at the 1928 Democratic Convention, and supported nominee Alfred E. Smith when most Georgians went for Hoover because Smith was a "wet" and a "Catholic." He supported most of the New Deal, including NRA, REA, TVA, SEC, and all the farm programs, and helped draft the Social Security Act.

There were, however, measures and actions which he did not support, leading to confrontation with the President. He opposed the Wages and Hours Act and the proposed plan to "pack" the Supreme Court. This caused President Roosevelt to go to Georgia in 1938 and call on the voters to "purge" George from the Senate. George's face-to-face declaration that, "I accept the challenge," and his subsequent triumph in the bitter, two-pronged challenge from Roosevelt's candidate, Lawrence Camp, on the left and Georgia's fire-eating former

73

Governor Eugene Talmadge on the right, propelled him into a position of national legislative prominence and power. Neither Roosevelt nor any subsequent President ever tried again to challenge him directly.

From that time until the day in 1956 that failing health forced him to concede his inability to face a contest for his seat against Ole Gene Talmadge's high-riding son, Herman — who was making issues of George's support of "foreign giveaways" and softness on segregation — he was acknowledged to be the most powerful man in America. In print he was referred to as the "Rock of the Senate." Together with his junior colleague, Richard Russell, he had more influence on the course of the nation's affairs at home and abroad than any of the presidents under whom they served.

Upon the announcement of his retirement, President Eisenhower named him his personal ambassador to the North Atlantic Treaty Organization in recognition of his unique status as "Statesman of the World." He occupied an office at the U. S. Department of State until his death less than a year after he stepped down from his Senate seat and post as President Pro Tempore of the Senate. A succession of coronary occlusions over a five-month period resulted in his death which occurred in his own bed in the modest bungalow home not far from the hamlet where he made his first speech or the beautiful lake on the Chattahoochee River which now bears his name.

Asked during his later years to characterize the source of his success and influence as a solon and a statesman, he replied with the quiet modesty for which he was noted: "It had not been my habit to fill the **Congressional Record** with speeches or even speak unless I had a real conviction one way or the other. If I have any influence in the Senate today, it is because the Senate has generally credited me with being sincere."

John Brown Gordon

(Lawyer, Writer, Lecturer, Miner, Industrialist, Major General in Confederate Army, twice Governor, three times United States Senator. Born February 6, 1832, Upson County, Georgia. Died Miami, Florida, January 9, 1904.)

John Brown Gordon was and is Georgia's "Man On A Horse." A true Renaissance Man of his time, he was highly successful in all of the many facets of his colorful career which were consistently characterized by both dignity and 'elan. It is appropriate that he is enshrined in memoriam by having the only equestrian statue on the grounds of the Georgia State Capitol.

A recurring anecdote of the Georgia General Assembly is about an inebriated member begging General Gordon to dismount and help him defeat a bill of questionable honesty. To which the General is said to respond: "I would be glad to do that, son, except they might steal my horse while I was gone." (The horse's name was Marye and she became Gordon's favorite mount after she ran riderless across Federal lines.)

The son of a preacher, Gordon was precocious and decisive in all that he did beginning with "joining the church" as a pre-schooler when he was so small he had to stand on a table to give his "confession" before the congregation. (That table is still a prized possession of the Grace Primitive Baptist Church in Thomaston.)

Young Gordon was so bright his father hired for him a tutor from Princeton, and he found the University of Georgia so unchallenging that he left to study law privately under the renowned Georgia Chief Justice-to-be Logan E. Bleckley. Finding that law did not satisfy him, he worked for a while as a newspaper correspondent before becoming manager of a coal mine in Dade County. While on a trip to Atlanta he met a

17-year-old girl from LaGrange, Fannie Haralson, who wore a gardenia in her hair. Within three weeks they were married. Theirs was a great and lasting love. They were so inseparable that Fannie followed him into battle during the Civil War and once fainted when she witnessed his being wounded.

When the Civil War began, Gordon was twenty-nine. Totally without military experience, he formed a company of mountaineers composed mostly of the men who worked in the mines he was overseeing. He called them "The Raccoon Roughs" because the only similarity in their uniforms were their coonskin caps. The Confederacy mustered them in as part of the Sixth Alabama Infantry Regiment and promoted Gordon from Captain to Lieutenant Colonel. From this rank he moved up rapidly to become successively Colonel, Brigadier General, and, on May 14, 1862, Major General.

By the end of the war Gordon was in command of half of The Army of Virginia and was under recommendation for promotion to Lieutenant General. He fought in many battles, led one of the daring charges at Gettysburg, and was credited with saving the life of General Robert E. Lee by stemming a break in the Confederate lines on May 12, 1864, at Spottsylvania.

Gordon was a pious man who sometimes was called "The Praying General." His men literally worshipped him, one reputed to have said, "Hit would put spirit into a whupped chicken just to look at him fight!" He was at Lee's side at Appomattox, and Douglas Southall Freeman wrote of him in **Lee's Lieutenants:** "If the final order of march had been arranged to honor those who had fought hardest and with highest distinction during the last days of the war, Gordon rightly would have been put first."

After the war, Gordon wrote his memoirs entitled **Reminiscenses** and became one of the first public figures to find the lecture circuit profitable. His most popular lecture, "The Last Days of the Confederacy," was widely acclaimed. One reviewing reporter wrote of his performance: "His voice had the clarity of a trumpet, and the charm of the flute. He used no useless gestures." One report from New England told of a Northerner who had lost a son in the war, saying to Gordon: "I have hated you all these years because of my dead boy. But when I heard you tell about the sufferings of the Southern boys, and their dying, I realized that they, too, were fighting for what they thought was right." Gordon owned a black body servant named Jim who accompanied him to the war and remained with him even after being freed. The General sent Jim's sons to college, and one of his grandsons later became governor of the Virgin Islands. Gordon also reputedly became head of the Ku Klux Klan in Georgia immediately following the Civil War. That never was documented, however, and he never admitted to its truth.

Evidence of the high esteem in which he was held by his fellow Georgians, Gordon was elected over the beloved Alexander Hamilton Stephens to the United States Senate in 1873 and was reelected in 1878. During this period Gordon became a member of the "Bourbon Triumvirate," along with former Governor and Chief Justice Joseph E. Brown and Governor Alfred H. Colquitt. In an arrangement which many, particularly the Independents led by Mrs. Rebecca Latimer Felton, charged was a "trade" or "deal," Gordon resigned his Senate seat in 1880 to accept a high-paying job with the railroads. Colquitt appointed Brown his successor in the Senate.

Historians are in dispute as to what actually happened. Such respected authorities as the late Dr. E. Merton Coulter say the criticism was "erroneously held," but it has been revealed that Gordon's friend, Henry W. Grady, did act as an intermediary with railroad magnate H. Victor Newcomb in arranging the details of Gordon's employment. Gordon's own explanation was that his family situation was such that he had to improve his finances and he did so by accepting the railroad job offer and branching into other businesses, particularly mining and lumbering. Whatever the facts, Georgians blamed Brown more than Gordon and subsequently elected Gordon governor for two terms and for a third time to the Senate.

Gordon was the first governor to occupy the new State Capitol, and how he became the State's Chief Executive is one of the more colorful stories of his career. Everyone had expected A. O. Bacon to be elected, but an event took place which caused a spontaneous outpouring of support for Gordon from former Confederate veterans. Bacon was overwhelmed. The phenomenon occurred at the unveiling of a statue in honor of the late Benjamin Harvey Hill. Program Chairman Henry W. Grady had arranged for the aging former President of the Confederacy, Jefferson Davis, to be the speaker. Davis came in the company of his daughter, but was too feeble to speak and asked Gordon to fill this role for him.

Davis and Gordon rode together in a parade through downtown Atlanta in a coach drawn by six white horses with 1,000 former Confederate soldiers marching behind and 6,000 school children throwing flowers in their path. At the site of the unveiling they were met by General James Longstreet who had come from his home in Gainesville. As the three former Confederate leaders embraced, the crowd went wild. Gordon delivered one of his greatest speeches, and he was on his way to the governor's chair.

Gordon was a good, but conservative, governor who acted decisively to put an end to abuses in the convict-leasing system in which his own companies were participants. He entertained the first Democratic President since the Civil War, Grover Cleveland, when he visited Atlanta. But he was embarrassed when one of his family retainers refused to meet the President after he requested to be introduced to a typical "Negro mammy" of the day. The elderly black lady had been with the Gordons in Washington, and she told the person sent to the farm to get her that she had a "misery in the leg" and besides, she had seen enough Presidents when she was in Washington. She later apologized to President Cleveland who reportedly was highly amused by the incident.

Gordon served as Governor from 1886 through 1890, and the following year was named to a third Senate term which he served in full. He died January 4, 1904, in Miami, Florida, after becoming ill while walking on the family farm with his grandson during a visit with his son, Hugh Haralson Gordon. His body was brought back to Atlanta where he was given a hero's burial only one week after the death of General Longstreet. An Atlanta newspaper of the day carried this headline: "Hats off! Gordon comes home today."

Gordon's unique statue was dedicated by Governor Joseph M. Terrell shortly before he left office in 1907. His memory also is honored by a county, town, and junior college which bear his name.

Henry Woodfin Grady

(Journalist, Lecturer, Editor of **The Atlanta Constitution,** *Scribe and Spokesman for "The New South." Born May 24, 1850, Athens, Georgia. Died December 23, 1889, Atlanta, Georgia.)*

The phrase "The New South" and the name Henry W. Grady are synonymous. While it can be debated either way that one was the product of the other, it is to Grady that the credit must go for putting into both the written and spoken word the substance of the term as it applied to both the facts and the promise of the region in the period following Reconstruction and preceding the turn of the century.

The term was first used by Grady as the title for his famous and brilliant address before the New England Society in New York City on December 22, 1886. In the address he publicly confronted General William Tecumseh Sherman for being "kind of careless with fire" and advised him and those in the fashionable audience at Delmonico's Restaurant that from the ashes he left "we have built a brave and beautiful city in Atlanta, that we have caught the sunshine in the brick and mortar of our homes, and have builded therein not one ignoble prejudice or memory."

Many historians date the renaissance of the South into what now has become the envied "Sunbelt" of the nation from that oration. Grady's eloquent words struck the spark of awareness in those who heard him that the conquered region of cotton and slavery was changing in both economic and philosophical orientation and would be a future national factor which must be recognized and reckoned with.

From that moment until his death from pneumonia contracted while making a similar speech in Boston three years later, Grady was in constant demand to carry the message of "The New South" throughout the nation. Upon his demise, contributions from throughout the nation — including one from Andrew Carnegie — paid for a statue of Grady which was unveiled on Henry Grady Square in the middle of Marietta Street in the shadow of the building housing **The Atlanta Constitution** and looking directly upon the Five Points area of his beloved Atlanta.

Born into a family descended from Irish immigrants who had changed their name from O'Grady, Henry proposed to his wife, Julia, at the age of twelve. They were married when she grew up and while he was getting an education at the University of Georgia. The nation's oldest chartered state university now has a famous School of Journalism and Mass Communications named for him. Grady subsequently studied law for two years at the University of Virginia.

His first job was as a reporter for **The Atlanta Constitution.** Stints as editor of two newspapers in Rome followed, the latter of which failed. He was also co-founder of the short-lived **Atlanta Herald.** In 1876 he became Georgia Correspondent for **The New York Herald** and an editorial writer for **The Atlanta Constitution.** He bought a quarter interest in **The Constitution** and became its managing editor in 1880.

From that moment on Grady worked, almost as if obsessed, for promotion of the agricultural development of the South and for better relations between the North and South. He was largely responsible for the Cotton Exposition of 1881 and the Piedmont Expositions of 1887 and 1889 in Atlanta. It was said the latter "drew together the largest multitude of people ever gathered in the South in a time of peace, and . . . was the most notable in many respects ever organized in the South." It also was in his office that the meeting was held which led to the establishment of the Georgia School of Technology.

Grady was instrumental in bringing to **The Atlanta Constitution** such distinguished literary figures as Joel Chandler Harris, originator of the "Uncle Remus" stories; Charles Henry Smith, the humorist and political satirist who wrote weekly "letters" under the name of Bill Arp; and Frank L. Stanton, whose "Mighty Lak' A Rose" and other poems was to make him Georgia's first poet laureate.

The noted editor and orator also was active in the politics of the "Bourbon Triumvirate" — Joseph Emerson Brown, Alfred H. Colquitt, and John B. Gordon — and their conservative policies founded upon economic and industrial development. He played key roles in the election of every Georgia governor and United States Senator during the '80's. He was particularly close to Gordon, a Confederate general and hero, and played a key role as go-between in the negotiations which led to Gordon's resignation as United States Senator and paved the way for the appointment of Brown. He also was in charge of the arrangements for the ceremony dedicating the statue honoring Benjamin Harvey Hill at which the tearful reunion of Ex-Confederate President Jefferson Davis, Confederate General James Longstreet, and Gordon took place. It was this dramatic meeting which provided the impetus that soon thereafter elevated Gordon to the governorship.

At the height of his acclaim, Grady was presented with a petition signed by thousands of Georgians urging him to be a candidate for an at-large seat in the U. S. Congress. Of this development, he said to one of his editorial assistants, "I shall have to pretend to consider this, but my mind is already made up." Shortly thereafter, a delegation from the State Legislature, many of them pledged by their constituents to vote for another man, called on him and urged him to become a candidate for the United States Senate. Grady steadfastly refused.

But it was in his columns and his speeches that he carried the word of the winds of change which were blowing across the South. With missionary zeal he worked to attract the infusion of northern capital and industrial know-how which the region needed to put the legacies of the Civil War behind it. It was said that "no one was more surprised" than he at the attention and acclaim attracted by his New York speech. While it was mainly extemporaneous and not fully reported, the widespread quotation from published excerpts was considered remarkable. He said he was "literally overwhelmed" by the outbursts of enthusiasm with which people praised him for making these statements during the course of the now famous address.

"We have found out that in the general summary the free Negro counts more than he did as a slave. We have sowed towns and cities in the place of theories and put business above politics. We have challenged your spinners in Massachusetts and your ironmakers in Pennsylvania. . . . We have learned that one northern immigrant is worth fifty foreigners, and have smoothed the path to southward, wiped out the place where Mason and Dixon's line used to be, and hung our latch-string to you and yours. . . . We have let economy take root and spread among us as rank as the crabgrass which spring from Sherman's Cavalry camps. . . .

"The Old South rested everything on slavery and agriculture, unconscious that these could neither give nor maintain healthy growth. The New South presents a perfect Democracy, the oligarchs leading in the popular movement — a social system compact and closely knitted, less splendid on the surface but stronger at the core — a hundred farms for every plantation, fifty homes for every palace, and a diversified industry that meets the needs of this complex age."

Among the scores of addresses he made during the remaining months of his life were those at the Texas State Fair Association in Dallas. Wherever he traveled, his train was mobbed at every stop. Of his oration before the literary societies of the University of Virginia where he had been a student, **The New York Sun** wrote that it was "full of poetry, but it deals with some very practical and serious issues. The felicity of the style, the apt and striking illustrations, the little bits of humor and pathos, and the happy combination of all these, merely emphasize the serious aim and purpose of the orator."

But it is perhaps his final speech that is the most quoted, the one he made in Boston where he contracted the pneumonia from which he died ten days later. It was about a dead man which focused dramatic attention upon the need for industrialization in the New South:

"I attended a funeral in a Georgia county. It was a poor, one-gallused fellow. They buried him in the midst of a marble quarry; they cut through solid marble to make his grave; yet the little tombstone they put above him was from Vermont. They buried him in the midst of a pine forest, but his pine coffin was imported from Cincinnati. They buried him within touch of an iron mine, but the nails in his coffin and the iron in the shovel that dug his grave were from Pittsburgh. They buried him near the best sheep-grazing country in the world, yet the wool in the coffin bands was brought from the North. They buried him in a New York coat, a Boston pair of shoes, a pair of breeches from Chicago, and a shirt from Cincinnati. Georgia furnished only the corpse and a hole in the ground."

Seven thousand attended Grady's funeral. **The New York Tribune** commented that "never was a private person so universally mourned." In addition to his statue, funds raised by public subscription in his honor also were used to establish in Atlanta one of the nation's foremost public and teaching facilities, Grady Memorial Hospital. Also named for Grady were a major high school in Atlanta and a county in South Georgia. Until the development of modern Atlanta's Peachtree

Center, of which he surely would have approved, the city's major hotel which dominated the site and was the focus of political activity in the state's capital city also bore his name. His grandson, Eugene Black, became head of the World Bank, following his grandfather's economic pioneering on a world scale.

Not long before his death, Grady was asked what was his highest ambition. "To have my friends love me and believe in me," he replied, and by his own yardstick his life and works were phenomenal successes.

Button Gwinnett

(Merchant, Planter, Member State Assembly, Delegate to Continental Congress, Signer of Declaration of Independence, President Council of Safety. Born 1732, Hatherly, Gloucestershire, England. Died May 19, 1777, Savannah, Georgia. Place of Burial Disputed.)

Like a brilliant comet which burns brightly for a brief time and then is gone so Button Gwinnett flashed across the Georgia scene for less than a decade before and during the early days of the Revolution.

He was a man of mystery and unanswered questions both in life and in death after a short, but colorful, public career. Not even his exact birthdate in England is known. Nor could his grave be found when Georgia sought to honor its three signers of the Declaration of Independence by re-interring their remains under Signer's Monument in Augusta. Even today there is considerable dispute as to whether the bones buried in the grave marked as his in Colonial Cemetery in Savannah are actually his. Some believe he was buried atop an Indian mound near his home on St. Catherines Island and that his bones were washed out to sea during a hurricane. Residents of that area of the Georgia Coast say two ghosts of Gwinnett haunt that barrier island, one on his horse returning from Philadelphia and the other at the helm of his boat, "Beggar's Benison."

Gwinnett's small, cramped signature is the rarest of those of signers of the Declaration of Independence, and the State of Georgia owns one of the few in existence. The authenticity of the likeness of the Gwinnett bust in the State Capitol also has been questioned, and an Atlanta bank contends it has the only authentic portrait of him, one which shows him to be grim, thin-lipped, and solemn-eyed with a sharp nose and receding hairline.

Gwinnett received his unusual first name from a cousin,

84

Barbara Button, who left him a small legacy. Before emigrating to the New World, he worked for a tea merchant whose daughter he married in Bristol, England. He came first to Charleston and then, in 1765, to Savannah where he achieved a reasonable degree of success as a general trader, selling everything from medicines to gold bars. Three years later he converted all of his property to cash and paid Mary Musgrove and her husband, Thomas Bosomworth, 5,250 pounds for a portion of St. Catherines Island. The purchase included cattle, horses, hogs, lumber, and a boat. With some slaves he also purchased, he established a plantation where he turned his attention to the production of indigo, rice, corn, and lumber —the staples of the region. He also built a fine home which was purchased and restored in 1929 by E. J. Noble who made a fortune with Life-Saver mints.

His contacts with the mainland were through the Port of Sunbury where he met and developed a strong friendship with Dr. Lyman Hall who lost no time in converting him to the Patriot cause. Prior to that time, he had little interest in public affairs, but in 1769 he was elected to the State Assembly. It is recorded that he was fined for tardiness on several occasions and that once an officer was sent to arrest him for being absent without leave, a charge which was withdrawn when it was learned he was ill.

The people of St. John's Parish elected him to represent them at the Second Provincial Congress in Savannah, and on February 1, 1776, he was named to succeed Noble Wymberly Jones as one of Georgia's five Delegates to the Continental Congress. But the terminal illness of Jones' father prevented his attendance. In Philadelphia, Gwinnett joined his friend, Dr. Hall, and George Walton as one of the three who signed the Declaration of Independence for Georgia on July 4, 1776.

At the direction of the Continental Congress, Gwinnett brought and presented to the Georgia Council of Safety a resolution authorizing Georgia to enlist a regiment of Rangers composed of one battalion each of horse and foot soldiers and two companies of artillery to garrison the forts at Savannah and Sunbury. He also relayed a resolution to construct four galleys for the defense of Georgia. All this was to be done at Georgia's expense but placed under the command of the central government.

He was successful in persuading the Council to take those actions, and on October 7, 1776, he was named a member of the Council while retaining his position as Delegate to the

Continental Congress. Council President Archibald Bulloch named him his Assistant and assigned him to the committee to draft Georgia's first state constitution.

With Gwinnett taking the leading role, the committee produced a constitution of sixty-three articles during the winter of 1776-77. The document was ratified in February 1777 by a convention called by President Bulloch. Gwinnett generally is credited with being the "father" of that Constitution which lasted for twelve years. It contained some interesting provisions attributed to him, including the establishment of a unicameral State Legislature, the requirement that schools be erected in each county and "supported at the general expense of the state," and the provision for a weak governor limited to a one-year term who was required to swear that he would not attempt to "hold over" in office. Credit for the design of the first official seal which was adopted by the same convention also is given to Gwinnett.

As the state prepared to implement the Constitution with the election of its first Governor, Bulloch — who was greatly revered and was expected to be named to that post without opposition — suddenly died. The Council then named Gwinnett to serve as Acting President in a resolution addressing him as "Our Trusty and Well-Beloved Button Gwinnett" and Gwinnett now launched his own campaign for the honor of being Georgia's first chief executive. To his surprise and disappointment, however, he was soundly defeated by the hardy old Salzburger, John Adam Treutlen, largely due to the opposition of the Scotch Highlanders of Darien. They were led by the McIntosh Clan which controlled enough votes to determine the outcome of the election.

Gwinnett's enmity for the McIntoshes, particularly General Lachlan McIntosh, had its beginning when McIntosh was chosen by the Continental Congress instead of Gwinnett to be Commander of the forces of the Continental Army in Georgia. Gwinnett felt the appointment should have gone to him in recognition of his being a signer of the Declaration of Independence and his success in persuading the Council of Safety to raise and support the troops McIntosh would command. When he became Acting President of the Council and Commander-in-Chief of Georgia, Gwinnett proceeded to ignore McIntosh and planned an expedition against the British in Florida which failed when Colonel Samuel Elbert, McIntosh's second in command, told him of the plans. McIntosh then led his own expedition into Florida. This was also a failure. When the

Council called both men before it to explain, heated words were exchanged, with McIntosh calling Gwinnett a "rotten-hearted, lying scoundrel." Even Gwinnett's friend and co-signer, George Walton, was prompted to comment that Gwinnett, "like Alexander the Great, imagines himself to be lord of the earth."

A further bone of contention between Gwinnett and the McIntoshes arose when Gwinnett had Lachlan's younger brother, George, arrested and put into irons after receiving a letter from President John Hancock of the Continental Congress informing him that George McIntosh was suspected of trading with the British in Florida. Although young McIntosh was also a member of the Council of Safety, Gwinnett denied him bail; and, when he finally won his release and exonerated himself before the Continental Congress, he vowed revenge.

When Lachlan McIntosh expressed delight over Gwinnett's defeat and claimed credit for it, Gwinnett challenged him to a duel which was fought at dawn on May 15, 1777 inside the city limits of Savannah. Both men were wounded in the leg, Gwinnett the most seriously with his hip broken. When McIntosh inquired, "Do you want another shot?" Gwinnett said, "Yes, if somebody will help me up." But the seconds stopped the contest and the men shook hands. Gwinnett died four days later of gangrene. At the insistence of his fellow co-signers Hall and Walton, McIntosh was indicted and tried. Following acquittal, he was exiled to military assignments outside Georgia, including a winter with Washington at Valley Forge, until late in the war. Mrs. Gwinnett unsuccessfully sought redress and compensation from the Continental Congress, shortly moving with her son to South Carolina where both died not long afterwards, leaving no descendants.

Gwinnett thus was forgotten until the search was made for his grave in 1848, and there now exists no authentic records on the disposition and location of his remains. A thigh bone later claimed to be his subsequently was proven to be that of a teen-aged female.

His biographer, Charles C. Jones, wrote that Gwinnett's name is "inseparably associated . . . with the charter of American independence" and goes on to conclude about his flawed and unfulfilled life: "Of his intelligence, force of character, ability to command success, courage, indomitable will, tenacity of purpose, patriotism, love of liberty, and devotion to the cause of American freedom, he gave proof most abundant. But he was ambitious, covetous of power, strong in his prejudices, intolerant of opposition, and violent in his hate."

James Habersham (Father)

(Wealthy Merchant and Planter, Secretary and Acting Governor of Colony of Georgia. Born January 1713, Beverly, Yorkshire, England. Died August 18, 1775, New Brunswick, New Jersey.)

Joseph Habersham (Son)

(Leader of Liberty Boys, Colonel in Continental Army, Speaker of Georgia General Assembly, Mayor of Savannah, First Postmaster General of United States. Born July 28, 1751. Died November 17, 1815, Savannah, Georgia.)

James Habersham's biographer, Otis Ashmore, feels his death before the American Revolution "was fortunate for him" because of what he had written a friend in England several months earlier. Although he did not approve of King George's various taxes which had provoked the colonists, Habersham said, "I would not chuse (sic) to live here longer than we are in a state of proper subordination to, and under the protection of Great Britain."

And it certainly was just as well that he never knew of the leadership role his son Joseph played in fomenting and carrying out that Revolution, particularly as one of the Liberty Boys of Savannah. It was the younger Habersham who led the group in stealing the King's ammunition from the stores of his father's friend, Royal Governor James Wright, and shipping it to Patriots in New England for use in the Battle of Bunker Hill.

This episode took place about the same time James Habersham departed Georgia for Philadelphia and New Brunswick, New Jersey, where he died seeking recovery of his health in his long, agonizing fight against the ravages of gout.

James Habersham was a man of conscience who was converted by the spellbinding evangelist George Whitefield, the Billy Graham of his day. After his conversion, Habersham turned his back on a fortune in England to join Whitefield in a tortuous immigration to the Colony of Georgia to establish and conduct an orphanage and school for poor children. Bethesda, the institution they founded and nurtured to permanence and prominence, continues to exist today on the Isle of Hope near Savannah. The first orphanage in the New World has attracted the philanthropies of the great and near great through the years. One of its earliest supporters was Benjamin Franklin who wrote that under the sway of one of Whitefield's moving sermons, he "emptied my pockets into the collection dish, gold and all," Franklin later became a Bethesda Trustee.

Because he was a learned and righteous man, James Habersham's advice often was sought by the early colonists. Although at times he was in contention with General Oglethorpe and the magistrates of the Colony, his judgment and leadership were vindicated by the success of certain of his ideas. Among these was the abandonment of silk culture and small farms in favor of cotton and rice plantations operated by slave labor. Habersham's own holdings and farming efforts made him a wealthy man for the second time in his life, he having the distinction of raising and exporting the first cotton ever shipped from America.

With his friend Francis Harris he established Harris and Habersham, Savannah's first commercial enterprise, in 1774. The firm soon was conducting commerce in pitch, tar, rice, peltry, indigo, and later cotton not only with the Northern Colonies but also with London.

He was appointed Secretary of the Colony and Royal Councillor by Governor Wright and was elected President of the Upper House of the General Assembly. From the latter post he was chosen by Governor Wright to serve as Acting Governor for nineteen months while Wright went to England on leave of absence. It was during this period that he twice refused to recognize the election of the Patriot, Dr. Nobel Wymberly Jones, as Speaker of the House of Representatives and dissolved the Assembly when it refused to expunge a third, though declined, election from the record.

Habersham foresaw trouble coming and warned the British of the consequences of their actions, stating, "If you persist in your right to tax the colonists, you will drive them to rebellion." But he remained steadfastly loyal to the crown and died a loyal subject of King George II.

Joseph Habersham, like his brothers, was educated at Princeton. Both he and his brother John were prominent in the rebellion before and after the Declaration of Independence. He was a leader in the formation of the Liberty Boys, Savannah's branch of the Sons of Liberty which had its beginning in New England and spread throughout the colonies. The younger Habersham was a principal spokesman when the group met at Tondee's Tavern and erected their famous Liberty Pole. Older colonists called the young activists "Liberty Brawlers" and Governor Wright dubbed them "Sons of Licentiousness."

The Liberty Boys resolved there would be no stamps sold in Georgia, spiked the city's cannon so no salute could be fired at the annual celebration of the King's birthday and hanged the governor in effigy. They made their point to the extent that when the King's Stampseller, George Angus, arrived on January 6, 1766, Governor Wright assigned forty British Rangers to guard him. Angus became so frightened and intimidated that he took his stamps and left on February 8 on the same ship on which he had arrived. He had sold only seventy stamps, all of which went for clearance of a ship which had to sail because of its perishable cargo. That was the end of the Stamp Act in Georgia, and it subsequently was repealed by Parliament on July 16 of that year.

When news of the Battles of Lexington and Concord reached Georgia, the Liberty Boys on May 10, 1775, broke into the King's Ammunition Stores which Governor Wright had secured east of Savannah in an unguarded brick bunker twelve feet underground. They shipped most of the contents to Boston where it later was used by the men of General Benjamin Lincoln in the Battle of Bunker Hill. The feat had been accomplished under the leadership of Joseph Habersham, James Jackson, John Milledge, and Edward Telfair. Habersham would be named First Postmaster General of the United States by President Washington and his three companions were to be governors of Georgia. (Lincoln later would lead the army which fought to liberate Georgia from the British.) Governor Wright ranted and fumed over the escapade and offered a reward of 150 pounds for information on the identity of the rebels. Although many knew who were responsible, not a soul sought the reward.

John Glynn was elected President of Georgia's first Provincial Congress which assembled on August 10, 1774. The gathering was less than successful because of the harassment and counter efforts of Governor Wright and his followers. It was their opposition that thwarted the sending of official delegates to the First Continental Congress at Philadelphia.

Ten months later, on June 22, 1775, Habersham and the Liberty Boys met again at Tondee's Tavern and organized a Council of Safety to govern the colony. William Ewen was elected President. Among those in attendance was Francis Harris, the partner of Joseph's father. The meeting was highlighted by the drinking of thirteen toasts, one to each of the thirteen colonies, and the hoisting of a Union Flag on the Liberty Pole. A sailor named John Hopkins, who happened by and made some impertinent remarks, was tarred and feathered, made to kiss the Liberty Pole, and forced to apologize by saying, "Damnation to all Tories and success to the cause of American liberty!" A call was issued for a Second Provincial Congress for July 4, 1775, at which all twelve of Georgia's parishes were represented. Archibald Bulloch was elected President and he, Lyman Hall, John Houstoun, Noble Wymberly Jones, and Rev. Joachim Zubly were named official delegates to the Second Continental Congress.

The Liberty Boys formed their own battalion and named General Lachlan McIntosh as their Commander, Samuel Elbert as Chief Aide with the rank of Lieutenant Colonel, and Joseph Habersham as Major and third in command. Joseph also was commissioned by the Georgia Provincial Congress to command a Georgia Navy and to take charge of whatever ships and naval defenses the colony might later have or establish. General Charles Lee of Charleston (no relation to the Virginia Lees) was the American commander in the South. When he came to Savannah to review Georgia's troops and defenses in early 1776, he was dismayed and thought the Georgians had an exaggerated notion of their fighting capacities and abilities. Of them he wrote: "These Georgians would tackle anything. They propose to defend their frontier with Horse Rangers, and it turns out that they do not have there a single horse. Later, they planned to defend it by boats — and they had no boats! I would not be surprised to hear them propose to defend the coastal country with mermaids mounted on alligators!"

On January 18, 1776, the Council of Safety adopted a resolution calling for the arrest of Governor Wright and his aides and assigned Joseph, then twenty-four to do the job. He and his men went to the Governor's office where he laid his hand on Wright's shoulder and declared, "Sir James, you are my prisoner." The Council members fled and the Governor was allowed to remain under house arrest until he escaped to a British ship and sailed to Nova Scotia on February 11, 1776.

Joseph served throughout the war, advancing to the rank of Colonel before its conclusion. He served in the Continental Congress and the Georgia Convention that ratified the United States Constitution, was Speaker of the Georgia House of Representatives, Assistant Justice of Chatham County, Mayor of Savannah, and the First Postmaster General of the United States. When President Washington made his much-heralded visit to Georgia in 1791, Colonel Joseph Habersham was one of his hosts and escorts.

Habersham County is named in his honor and, of course, his family name is known to every Georgia school child from recitations of Sidney Lanier's immortal poem, "Song of the Chattahoochee."

Lyman Hall

(Physician, Leader of Georgia Puritans, Delegate to Continental Congress, Signer of Declaration of Independence, Governor. Born April 12, 1724, Wallingford, Connecticut. Died October 19, 1790, Burke County, Georgia. Buried under Signer's Monument, Augusta, Georgia.)

Lyman Hall never bore arms nor engaged in political oratory, but his handsome countenance, six-foot stature, personal grace and charm, and great force of character inspired confidence. For these reasons, the Puritans of Midway — those passionate Patriots who later named their county for the liberty for which they fought — would have followed him anywhere.

When their fellow Georgians dillydallied about sending representatives to the Continental Congress, the Puritans named Dr. Hall their delegate and dispatched him to Philadelphia. With him they sent 150 barrels of rice and fifty British Pounds for the relief of the suffering in Massachusetts. Hall was seated as a non-voting, but participating, delegate whose role was portrayed in the award-winning Broadway Musical "1776" in 1970. When Georgia did send a delegation, Hall was named one of its members, and he was one of the three Georgians who signed the Declaration of Independence.

Born in Wallingford, Connecticut, in the fifth generation of a family whose paternal ancestor came from England on the ship Griffin, Hall was a brilliant student who was graduated from Yale College after switching from the study of theology to medicine. He came south — first to Dorchester, South Carolina, and then to Midway (so named because it was halfway between Savannah and Darien) in what is now Liberty County — to

93

be physician to the Puritan settlers there. His services were much in demand due to the sicknesses emanating from the malarial swamps of the area.

Hall established two homes, one at the port of Sunbury and the other a plantation, Hall's Knoll, located north of Midway Meeting House, a Congregational church which he joined and of which he became a leader. Many of his possessions, including his pistols, can be seen today in the Midway Museum located near the church. He rapidly became not only the leading physician of the area but, due to his sympathetic nature, politeness, learning, and honest judgment, the leader in public affairs as well. He took the side of the Patriots when the clouds of the Revolution began to gather, and of him Colonel C. C. Jones was to say:

"On the revolutionary altars erected within the Midway District were the fires of resistance to the dominion of England earliest kindled; and of all the patriots of that uncompromising community, Lyman Hall, by his counsel, exhortations, and determined spirit, added stoutest fuel to the flames."

The pro-secession activities of Hall and his followers provoked Royal Governor James Wright to denounce them as "those meddlesome Puritans at Midway." The Puritans, in turn, became so frustrated with the inaction of their fellow Georgians that they voted to secede from Georgia and sent Dr. Hall to Charleston to discuss the possibility of annexation to South Carolina. The leaders of the neighboring colony, declined to become involved but did agree to recommend that the Continental Congress recognize the Puritans. Their feelings were assuaged, however, when Georgia finally did appoint a delegation and named Dr. Hall, already in Philadelphia, as one of its members.

Following signing of the Declaration, he returned to Georgia to great acclaim and sided with his co-signer, Button Gwinnett, in the controversy with General Lachlan McIntosh over conduct of the war. The conflict resulted in the duel in which Gwinnett was fatally wounded, and Hall was one of the leaders of the movement to press charges against McIntosh, charges from which he subsequently was acquitted.

Hall had to flee north when the invading British troops sought to capture and punish him. They burned his house at Sunbury, despoiled his plantation at Midway and confiscated all of his property. He removed his wife and family to Philadelphia where they remained until 1782 when they returned to Georgia to settle in Savannah. There he resumed his medical practice and set about repairing his shattered fortune.

In 1783 Hall was elected Governor of Georgia and became the first in that weak office to attempt to exercise strong executive leadership. In his message to the General Assembly on July 8, 1783, he proposed a program of public schools, the establishment of a university, the reorganization and repair of churches, the negotiation of land treaties with the Indians, the revision of the state's land laws, and improvement of the state's finances and military status. In his unprecedented "State of the State" address, he declared:

"In addition, therefore, to wholesome laws restraining vice, every encouragement ought to be given to introduce religion, and learned clergy to perform divine worship in honor of God, and to cultivate principles of religion and virtue among our citizens. For this purpose, it will be your wisdom to lay an early foundation for endowing seminaries of learning; nor can you, I conceive, lay a better than by a grant of a sufficient tract of land, that may, as in other governments, hereafter, by lease or otherwise, raise a revenue sufficient to support such valuable institutions."

The Assembly responded by voting to confiscate the property of those who sided with England and provided that the land and proceeds would go for the establishment and support of schools. It also created boards of commissioners for Richmond, Wilkes, and Burke Counties and authorized them to lay out county seats, sell lots, build academies, and oversee their operation.

As a result of these actions, within two years Richmond Academy, Georgia's oldest public school, opened, and the University of Georgia was chartered with a grant of 40,000 acres of land for its support. Hall worked particularly hard in conjunction with his fellow Yale alumni, Abraham Baldwin and Dr. Nathan Brownson, on the University's charter, but he did not live to see it begin operation. His plea for church support culminated in the enactment of a law two years later, which never was implemented, to provide for county ministers elected by the voters and paid by the state with all denominations having "equal toleration."

Upon the completion of his term of office at the State Capitol in Augusta, Dr. Hall returned to Savannah and again took up the practice of medicine. He also was elected Judge of the Inferior Court of Chatham County, a position he resigned in 1790 when he purchased a large plantation near Shell Bluff on the Savannah River in Burke County. There he engaged in extensive farming operations until his death at the age of sixty-seven on October 19, 1790.

Hall was buried in a brick vault overlooking the river. In 1848 his remains and those of his Declaration co-signer, George Walton, were re-interred with honors under Signer's Monument erected in Augusta in tribute to the three adopted sons who signed the Declaration of Independence for Georgia. (The remains of Button Gwinnett could not be located at the time and remain unauthenticated to date.)

The marble slab which marked the vault in which Dr. Hall originally was buried was sent to Wallingford, Connecticut, where it has been preserved as a monument to his memory there.

His biographer, Otis Ashmore, concluded that Hall's success and popularity were due to the combination of his gentle nature and great courage under the influence of which "the people felt safe with his hand at the helm."

Joel Chandler Harris

(Journalist, New South Writer, Master of Negro Dialect and Folklore, Author of "Uncle Remus" Stories. Born December 9, 1848, near Eatonton, Georgia. Died July 3, 1908, Atlanta, Georgia.)

Joel Chandler Harris would have been mortified to the quick of his sensitive soul had he lived to see his gentle tales of black folklore and masterful characterizations of Negro dialect denounced as prejudiced in concept and racist in motivation as they have been. With the possible exception of his friend and compatriot, Henry W. Grady, no Georgian of his time was more outspoken in calling for racial harmony and dismissing as a "bugaboo" the white fear of integration and social equality than he.

Obviously he conveyed no bigotry to his children because his son and daughter-in-law, Julian LaRose and Julia Collier Harris, were the first Georgians to win a Pulitzer Prize for their courageous crusade against the terrorist activities of the Ku Klux Klan through the editorial columns of their newspaper, the **Columbus Enquirer-Sun.** And of all people, Harris probably had more personal incentive than anyone before or since to oppose discrimination and demeaning of others in all forms inasmuch as he, from his earliest years, had had to endure epithets like "red-headed bastard" and all the other taunts hurled against an introverted, stuttering, undersized, red-haired, freckled lad who never knew the Irish father who deserted his high-minded seamstress mother before he was born.

Criticism of Harris and his works came in the wake of the civil rights crusades of the 1950's and 60's, some three-quarters of a century after the man who has been called "Georgia's Aesop" created his sage, black teller of children's fables, "Uncle Remus," and his stories of "Br'er Rabbit," "Br'er Fox," and his whole cast of both delightful and despicable personified animal characters. The stories were translated into twenty-seven languages and circulated worldwide to the delight of generations of children (and adults) everywhere. Prior to that time, Harris was credited with being the first of the writers of his era to "humanize" blacks as well as to portray poor whites as more than "white trash."

Frank L. Stanton, Georgia's first poet laureate, was his contemporary and friend from the days they both worked for the same papers in Savannah and Atlanta. Of Harris and his stories, Stanton said that "he made the lowly cabin-fires light the far windows of the world." The great Walt Disney translated his stories to film in his widely-acclaimed animated feature, "Song of the South." He also was ahead of his time in espousing equality of the sexes, one of his famous and often-quoted editorial paragraphs stating, "Man is not the intellectual superior of woman, else why does he unbosom his trials and troubles to his wife and mother?"

Harris' literary-minded mother read to him from the classics and encouraged him to compose little stories. He later wrote that his desire "to write — to give expression to my thoughts —grew out of hearing my mother read **The Vicar of Wakefield."** So at the age of thirteen he answered an advertisement for "an active, intelligent white boy, fourteen or fifteen years of age . . . to learn the printing business" and became a protege of Joseph Addison Turner who printed the short-lived, but widely-acclaimed quarterly, **The Plantation,** on his plantation near Eatonton.

It was there that Harris learned the printing trade and immersed himself in the books which an admiring Turner loaned him from his extensive library. He spent his evening hours in the company of the plantation slaves, listening to the singing of their rich spirituals, absorbing the colorful dialect of the black workers, and drinking in the original tales and fables spun by the patriarch of the plantation, "Uncle George" Terrell, whom many believe to have been the prototype of "Uncle Remus." Harris, however, claimed the character was an amalgam of many individuals, one of whom he identified as "Uncle Joe" Capers, the driver of the stagecoach which went through Eatonton.

Harris left the Turner Plantation in advance of General Sherman's hordes who wasted it and put Turner's magazine out of business. He went to Macon where he worked as a printer for **The Macon Telegraph** until he no longer could stand the antics of co-workers who would get him drunk to hear him stutter. From Macon he moved to New Orleans where he worked for six months as secretary to the publisher of **The Crescent Monthly** before returning to Georgia and **The Monroe Advertiser** in Forsyth.

Harris' pithy, humorous, editorial paragraphs attracted the attention of **The Savannah News.** He became the paper's Associate Editor and in the port city met his future wife, Esther du Pont LaRose, daughter of a French-Canadian sea captain, whom he wooed and won through writing and sending her romantic poems.

In 1876 they and "two bow-legged children and a bilious nurse" fled to Atlanta to escape the Yellow Fever Epidemic. There he found work as an editorial writer on **The Atlanta Constitution** and invented "Uncle Remus" one gloomy January day to overcome a case of "writer's block." His witty paragraphs had ceased to flow. In desperation he wrote a dialect column about how "Br'er Rabbit" accepted a dinner invitation from "Br'er Fox" only to find himself slated to be the main course and how he outwitted him. The tale brought a flood of enthusiastic letters from readers. As a result, the Managing Editor and soon-to-be-publisher, Captain Evan P. Howell, asked Harris to revive the Negro dialect stories which Sam Small, who had departed for another paper, had been writing under the pen name of Uncle Si. This Harris did, using the name "Uncle Remus" and calling on his store of tales learned on the plantation. This marked the beginning, at the age of thirty-two, of fifteen years of writings which were to make him a worldwide celebrity. His columns were syndicated to northern and western newspapers and were compiled into a series of "Uncle Remus" books, beginning with **Uncle Remus: His Songs and His Sayings** (1880).

Still shy and retiring, Harris built his home, "Wren's Nest," which now is a museum filled with his memorabilia. It was located on "Snap Bean Farm" in Atlanta's West End. The name for his home originated when a family of wrens took refuge and built its nest in the Harris mailbox and he dared anyone, including the postman, to disturb them. It was at the "Wren's Nest" that he did all of his later writing, including his autobiographical and other novels and many short stories. The only time he ventured out was to go to **The Constitution's** offices to write his editorials.

When President Theodore Roosevelt made his visit to Atlanta in 1905 and requested the honor of meeting Harris, then

Publisher Clark Howell, Sr. had to assign three reporters physically to escort Harris to the train with instructions "see that he's there if you have to hog-tie him." On another visit when Harris was supposed to stand in the receiving line with the President at the Governor's Mansion, he ducked in a side door and mingled with the crowd while Roosevelt greeted the guests. It took all the persuasion his wife and friends could muster to get him to accept the President's invitation to visit him at the White House.

Throughout the remainder of his life Harris continued to live quietly, doing his writing and tending his garden at "Wren's Nest." **A Dictionary of American Biography** described his life thusly: "Twenty-eight years of literary fame could not alter his habits, which were those of a sedate, home-loving country journalist, or change his appearance which corresponded to his habits." One of those habits was the wearing of a black felt hat, some said to hide his red hair and to discourage his being called "Carrot Top," which he never removed except for meals and bed and without which he never was photographed. He and his son Julian, the youngest of six children and one of three to survive infancy, established **Uncle Remus Magazine** in his later years; but, for an internationally-famous celebrity he died relatively broke, leaving only his home, $15,000 in insurance, royalties from his publications, and his interest in the magazine.

His family vetoed public requests that a statue be erected in his memory, his wife recalling that he often had said, "Don't erect any statue of marble or bronze to me to stand out in the rain and cold and dust." He was baptized into his wife's Catholic faith two weeks before his death at the age of fifty-nine and penned his own epitaph which appears on his grave in Atlanta's Westview Cemetery:

"I seem to see before me the smiling faces of thousands of children — some young and fresh — and some wearing the friendly marks of age, but all children at heart, and not an unfriendly face among them. And while I am trying hard to speak the right word, I seem to hear a voice lifted above the rest, saying, 'You have made some of us happy.' And so I feel my heart fluttering and my lips trembling and I have to bow silently and turn away and hurry into the obscurity that fits me best."

Nancy Morgan Hart

(Pioneer Woman. Heroine of American Revolution. Probably born in North Carolina, date unknown. Date of death unknown. Buried in Henderson County, Kentucky.)

Historians never have been able to separate fact from fable in recording the legendary exploits of Nancy Morgan Hart, the red-haired, rough-tongued, six-foot virago who was the scourge of the Tories and British on the Georgia frontier during the American Revolution. Very much in dispute is whether she was or was not cross-eyed and homely in appearance. All of the stories about her insist that she was both and her relatives maintain she was neither, the latter citing portraits which also are of questionable authenticity. But one conclusion is clear and that is, with the exception of the fact that she was no saint, her deeds of valor in conflict with the enemy are equal in every respect to those of Joan of Arc.

Few facts are known of her origin and early years. She was born into the well-known Morgan family which had Old Dominion roots, probably in North Carolina, and was a cousin to both Daniel Boone and Revolutionary War General Daniel Morgan. She married Benjamin Hart whose family produced both a Senator, Thomas Hart Benton of Missouri, and the wife of another famous Senator, Henry Clay of Kentucky.

The Harts took their vows in Orange County, North Carolina, and subsequently moved to 400 acres on the Broad River near Elberton, Georgia. On the land which had been granted to Benjamin he built a one-room log cabin and began wresting a hardscrabble living from the soil under the whip of Nancy's sharp tongue. His produce was supplemented by Nancy's marksmanship, as evidenced by the large number of impressive antlers which decorated the cabin. Taking note, visitors concluded that Nancy obviously "wore the pants in the family." One neighbor is quoted as saying, "Poor Nancy, she was a honey of a Patriot, but the devil of a wife"; and Nancy herself referred to Benjamin as "a poor stick." But that clearly did not interfere with their conjugal relationship which produced six sons and two daughters. It also won the respect of her Indian neighbors who called her "Warwoman" and gave that name, still in use, to a nearby creek.

The most generally accepted description of Nancy is the one that was published by a Milledgeville newspaper in 1825:

"In altitude, Mrs. Hart was almost Patagonian, remarkably well-limbed and muscular, and marked by nature with prominent features. She possessed none of those graces of motion which a poetical eye might see in the heave of the ocean wave or in the change of the summer cloud; nor did her cheeks — I will not speak of her nose — exhibit the rosy tints which dwell on the brow of the evening or play on the gilded bow. No one claims for her throat that it was lined with fiddlestrings. That dreadful scourge of beauty, the small-pox, had set its seal upon her face. She was called a hard swearer, was cross-eyed and cross-grained, but was nevertheless a sharp-shooter. Nothing was more common than to see her in full pursuit of the stag. The huge antlers which hung around her cabin, or upheld her trusty gun, gave proof of her skill in gunnery; and the white comb drained of its honey and hung up for ornament, testified to her powers in bee finding. Many bear witness to her magical art in the mazes of cookery, for she was able to prepare a pumpkin in as many ways as there are days in the week. She was extensively known and employed for her knowledge in the treatment of various kinds of ailments. But her skill took an even wider range, for the fact is well known that she held a tract of land by the safe tenure of a first survey, which was made on the Sabbath, hatchet in hand."

Nancy loved freedom, despised the British, and bore unrelenting hatred for their American sympathizers called Tories. When the British succeeded in capturing Savannah and Augusta and were advancing north and west to take the hinterlands, Nancy refused to let herself or her family be evacuated beyond the Blue Ridge Mountains as were most of her neighbors. Instead she stayed in her cabin which became a refuge for Patriots and offered her services as a fighter and a spy to her friend and neighbor, General Elijah Clarke.

On more than one occasion the legendary heroine disguised herself as a man and, pretending to be crazy, infiltrated British camps. From these forays she brought back much useful information for General Clarke about their numbers, armaments, and placements. When Clarke needed intelligence about the whereabouts and intentions of British Colonel Thomas Boyd who was marching into Georgia with 800 troops, Nancy fashioned a raft of logs tied with grapevines on which she crossed the Broad River. After scouting Boyd's strength and movements, she returned with data which enabled Clarke, General Andrew Pickens, and Colonel John Dooly to assemble a force of 500 Continentals and defeat Boyd in a surprise daylight attack at Kettle Creek. This was one of the few notable American victories in Georgia during the Revolutionary War. Both Nancy and Benjamin and their oldest son, Morgan, fought beside General Clarke in the encounter in which Boyd was fatally wounded, Clarke had a horse shot from under him, and Clarke's 13-year-old son, John, and the free black, Austin Dabney, were heroes.

On another occasion Nancy was left in charge of a fort while General Clarke and his men foraged for food. During their absence the fort was attacked by a band of Tories and Indians. But with the assistance of a young deserter whom she threatened with death, Nancy loaded and fired the fort's cannon and so frightened the attackers that they fled.

Her most famous exploit, however, was in single-handedly capturing and executing six Tories who descended upon her cabin to taunt her about allowing a Patriot to escape his pursuers by riding his horse through her cabin into the swamp behind it. Nancy boldly admitted her role, but feigned submission when the Tories shot her last yard turkey and demanded that she prepare a meal for them. She set about preparing a repast of the turkey, some venison, hoecake, pumpkin, and honeycomb. On the sly she sent her youngest daughter, Susie, who was called Sukey, to the spring for water with instructions to blow the conch shell kept on a nearby stump to summon her husband and his friends for assistance.

Lulled into complacency by Nancy's seeming meekness and the aroma of the good food, the Tories broke out a jug of whiskey and invited Nancy to partake. This she did with the declaration, "I'll take a swig with you, if it kills every cow on the island." All the while, as she was setting the table, she was taking their muskets one by one and pushing them outside through chinks in the cabin wall. When she called the men to the table, one of them saw her take the third of the five stacked weapons and challenged her. She immediately shouldered the gun and demanded that they "surrender their damned Tory carcasses to a Whig woman." One of the men charged her and she dropped him dead in his tracks. At this moment Sukey ran in from the spring and, sizing up the situation, quickly handed her mother one of the muskets she had pushed outside and announced, "Daddy and them will soon be here." Because of her supposedly crossed eyes, it appeared to each of the Tories that Nancy was personally aiming at him, and they hesitated rushing her as a group. When in desperation they did charge, she shot a second, wounding him, and the others agreed to surrender with the proposal that they "shake hands." Nancy held them at bay with a third weapon handed her by Sukey until Benjamin and his friends appeared. The men suggested shooting them all, but Nancy would have none of it, contending "shooting was too good for them." Under Nancy's gun, the Tories were marched outside the fence and all hanged, including the wounded man, to the tune of "Yankee Doodle."

For more than a century and a third the story was told without any conclusive proof of its truth. Then on December 12, 1912, a gang of workers grading the Elberton and Eastern Railroad unearthed the six skeletons in shallow graves three feet deep about half a mile from the site of Nancy's original cabin and thirteen miles from Elberton. **The Atlanta Constitution** reported the find, and it was considered conclusive proof that Nancy did indeed do what she said she had done.

It is generally believed that Nancy was in middle age at the time of the Revolutionary War. She and Benjamin continued to live on their land and raise their family until his death. Shortly thereafter, despite her advancing years and masculine character, she attracted a second and younger husband and trekked with him to the far western frontier where we lose track of the adventures of her later life. All that is known is that her last days were spent in Henderson County, Kentucky, probably with some of her Boone or Hart kin, and she was buried there upon her death.

Her life and exploits are commemorated in a number of ways. The Congress appropriated money for a monument to her memory which was erected on November 11, 1931, in Hartwell in Hart County, Georgia, both of which are named for her and which are the only county and county seat in the nation named for a woman. The Nancy Hart Highway which traverses the area also is the only highway in the United States named for a woman.

William Berry Hartsfield

(Lawyer, Member of Georgia House of Representatives, Alderman and Mayor of Atlanta, President of American Municipal Association. Born March 1, 1890. Died February 22, 1971.)

No more appropriate memorial ever has been established in memory of the leader of any era than the naming of the nation's busiest airport in honor of the colorful Atlanta mayor who was its father. Of all his accomplishments, William Berry Hartsfield was proudest of Atlanta's great international airport from which at peak periods more commercial aircraft take off and land daily than at any other aviation facility in the United States.

While in life Hartsfield never would agree to any city installation other than the incinerator being named in his honor, he doubtless would be pleased to know that Atlanta's Hartsfield International Airport, for which he picked the site as a youthful alderman during the years of aviation's infancy, bears his name. The fact that this ultra-modern hub of American aviation exists at a convenient location within a great metropolitan area is due to his foresight. It was upon his insistence that the City of Atlanta entered a lease-purchase agreement not only for the property on which the airport is located, at a time when everyone thought airplanes were the toys of rich playboys, but also the surrounding farmland for future expansion.

Bill Hartsfield became addicted to aviation as a high school dropout when he went to the racetrack owned by Coca-Cola magnate Asa Candler at Hapeville in 1909 to see the cars run. But he wound up being more fascinated by the aerial show put on by a French monoplane landing there. Later on he took lessons and learned to fly by himself.

Within fourteen years he had read law, been admitted to

the bar, was elected alderman from the Third Ward, and became Chairman of the City Council's new Aviation Committee charged with establishing a city airport. In that capacity, he persuaded Candler to give the city a five year lease-purchase agreement on the racetrack with a view toward establishing an airport, with the city paying the county taxes on it. Then he turned around and persuaded Fulton County to waive the taxes. In some further financial sleight of hand, he convinced the city to pay $1,000 for the adjacent land of a dairy farmer who complained the airplanes were causing his cows to go dry. Several years later the city would sell a portion of it for $400,000, leaving a net profit of $305,000 for use in building hangars and making other improvements when the racetrack was purchased for the agreed upon price of $94,000.

As a State Representative he subsequently sponsored the legislation authorizing cities and counties to operate airport facilities for lease to commercial airline operators. He further was successful in selling the Atlanta Chamber of Commerce on the importance of out-lobbying Birmingham in getting federal aviation authorities to designate Atlanta instead of Birmingham as the terminal and transfer point for the air routes being established between New York and Miami and Chicago and Jacksonville. He also was successful in getting an advanced night lighting system developed in Holland installed at the Atlanta Airport, making it an around-the-clock facility when night flying began in 1927.

Years later, as mayor, he convinced President Eisenhower to advocate a Federal Airport Construction Program under which Atlanta received funds for a modern terminal and expanded airport facilities. His love affair with the Atlanta Airport was one which continued throughout his long career of public service and on into his retirement years. Hartsfield's leadership was perhaps as much responsible for Atlanta becoming a modern, international city as any other factor.

Outside of Georgia Hartsfield was perhaps best known as a leader with progressive racial views who proclaimed his Atlanta to be a "city too busy to hate." A skillful practitioner of coalition politics which wedded the white business establishment and black voters, he integrated the Atlanta police force as early as 1948, taking the position that it would be difficult for civil rights cases to arise out of black officers enforcing the law against black violators. This he accomplished to the dismay of the white working classes led by dedicated opponents like Charlie Brown and Lester Maddox.

He also arranged for the arrest of leading black ministers so the state's bus segregation laws could be successfully challenged in federal courts. He integrated golf courses and swimming pools rather than close them. He defied segregationist Governor Marvin Griffin to plan and lead in the presence of invited news media from throughout the nation the peaceful integration of Atlanta public schools, declaring, "I don't give a damn what Griffin or anyone else said. I refuse to see Georgia go through another period of ignorance."

Hartsfield also was one of the successful challengers of Georgia's infamous county unit system which diluted populous Atlanta's voting clout in state elections. Because of these and other racial actions and his many outspoken statements on such subjects, his name was anathema to rural voters and politicians in Georgia. Being white, he perhaps was more cursed and despised than Martin Luther King, Jr., a fellow Atlantan with whom he often did not see eye-to-eye and whom he sometimes publicly criticized.

Although he championed Negro rights and led fearlessly in doing what he believed right for black citizens whose votes he assiduously courted, in his personal views Hartsfield was something less than a wholehearted integrationist. He often lashed out against "vilification and derision of Southern people, their customs and historic traditions" and once called on Congressman Martin Dies for an investigation of the role of the NAACP in "stirring up racial questions in the South."

In his continuing efforts to expand the Atlanta city limits, he blatantly raised the specter of a black majority city, once stating in a letter appealing to Citizens of Buckhead to vote themselves into Atlanta: "This is not intended to stir race prejudice because all of us want to deal fairly with them; but do you want to hand them political control of Atlanta?" He successfully opposed floridation of Atlanta's water until he left office and finally was muzzled by the Coca-Cola Company which had hired him as a consultant. He also fought daylight saving time.

Elected as a reform candidate in 1936, Hartsfield cleaned out corruption in the Police Deprtment and, with the help of his lifelong friend, Robert W. Woodruff, instituted budgetary and fiscal reforms which put the City in the black and kept it there with a surplus throughout his quarter of a century of service. Woodruff had lent his support to these efforts when he pledged the backing of Coca-Cola to the city's bankrupt treasury.

Hartsfield was defeated only once, in his bid for a second

term, when he lost by eighty-three votes to Roy LeCraw on the issue of the "hiding police" whom Hartsfield had put behind billboards to catch the speeders responsible for carnage on city streets. He retired in 1961 not because he feared defeat but because he wanted to divorce his wife to marry a beautiful, widowed former secretary.

He spent his last ten years of life earning more money than ever before, serving as President of the Southeastern Fair Association, as an active and salaried Mayor Emeritus, and as consultant to companies like Coca-Cola as well as philanthropic organizations like the Ford Foundation and the Rockefeller Brothers Fund. Also his friend, Bob Woodruff, whom he had first met when they were both starting out in business with the General Fire Extinguisher Company, occasionally would cut him in on a stock deal in which he would share in the profits without having to put up any money.

Hartsfield was particularly proud of his role in bringing the premiere of "Gone With The Wind" to Atlanta in 1939 and he made Margaret Mitchell Atlanta's History Advisor and Director of the Atlanta Centennial Celebration in 1948. As President and holder of other major posts in the American Municipal Association, he traveled throughout the world. He was known to the mayors of most of the cities in the Free World as well as to the leaders of their countries. He was acquainted with all the Presidents who held office contemporaneously with him and was said to be particularly dismayed that Franklin D. Roosevelt was the only one with whom he was never able to get a word in edgewise.

Hartsfield was an active mayor who kept a police radio in his car and personally went to the scene of every major fire, crime, or disturbance to see for himself what was going on and how it was handled. Because of his racial attitudes and activities, he received many threats, abusive letters, and telephone calls. For these reasons, he carried a pistol, rifle, and tear gas gun in his car at all times.

The Hartsfield temper was legendary, and he did not hesitate to go to the Atlanta newspapers and personally berate any reporter whose treatment of a story he questioned or to call Ralph McGill at home in the middle of the night. He once broke his hand pounding on the rail of the speaker's desk in the House of Representatives. On another occasion he climbed on the Clerk's desk to confront Speaker E. D. Rivers nose to nose. He was accused of many romantic involvements and, according to his biographer Harold Martin, in 1953 "went into the hospital for an operation that in the future would spare him the personal and political embarrassment of a possible paternity suit."

Upon the announcement of his retirement, **The Atlanta Journal** summed up Hartsfield and his career as follows: "He's got a hot temper, a stinging tongue, a strong will, a quick wit, a kind heart, a sense of history, a sense of destiny, a sense of humor, a capacity for growth, and a built-in finely tuned political radar set that seldom has failed him in his public life."

Benjamin Harvey Hill

 *(Lawyer, Orator, Member of Georgia House of Representatives, State Senator, Member of Provisional Congress of Confederate States of America, Confederate Senator, Member of U. S. Congress, United States Senator. Born September 14, 1823, Hillsborough, Georgia. Died August 16, 1882, Atlanta, Georgia.)*

All historians agree that Benjamin Harvey Hill was an orator without peer. "Silver-tongued" was the phrase used most often to describe his eloquence, although the late Bernice McCullar thought it should be "golden-tongued." According to one description, he was "a spellbinder, a man with gorgeous words, an orator of fire and thunder who could sing the voters to the polls." By any definition, however, his incomparable way with words was both the strength and weakness of his colorful legal and political career.

Hill's talent proved his undoing in his gubernatorial debates with the awkward and inarticulate Joe Brown. Audiences identified with Brown when Hill characterized him as "slow" and poked fun at the calico quilt some mountain ladies from his home county gave him as a campaign contribution. It also put him to the uncomfortable task of talking his way out of a challenge to a duel from Alexander Hamilton Stephens after "Little Aleck" took some of Hill's remarks in their debates on the 1856 presidential election to be an implication that he was a "Judas" to the Whig Party.

But his eloquence also rallied flagging Confederate morale in the latter days of the Civil War and endeared him forever in the hearts of Georgians and southerners. He further inspired southerners when he spoke out in the United States Congress against the fiery James G. Blaine after Blaine had made charges of inhumanity against Former Confederate President Jefferson Davis. During the war, Davis had said that Hill's pen and voice "were equal to ten thousand bayonets."

Hill was the son of a North Carolina dirt farmer for whom the hamlet of Hillsborough in Jasper County was named. He worked in the fields with his five brothers when the family moved into Indian Territory in what is now Troup County to scratch a farm out of the wilderness with their own hands and the labor of a few slaves.

Because of his aptitude for learning, his parents and a great aunt managed to scrape up $300 a year for three years to send him to the University of Georgia. He entered wearing home-made gray jeans and intent on making good his promise to graduate at the head of his class. After studying law for a year with William Dougherty, Hill was admitted to the bar. He married into the prominent Holt Family and moved to LaGrange where he set up a law practice. He became so prosperous that he bought his wife, Caroline, one of the finest homes in the city (now the LaGrange Woman's Club) and paid for it in two years. He later built another mansion on Prince Avenue in Athens, said to be one of the finest examples of antebellum architecture. The handsome structure has been preserved as the home of the President of the University of Georgia.

A conservative in philosophy and a Unionist in belief, Hill found his political place first in the Whig Party. Upon its demise, he joined the American or Know-Nothing Party. He served in the Georgia House of Representatives in 1851-52 and headed the campaign for Millard Fillmore and the American Party Ticket in 1856. This led to the fractious, five-hour debate in which historians agree that "Stephens more than met his match in Hill." It culminated in a demand for satisfaction from Stephens which Hill also successfully sidestepped with a "rollicking sarcastic answer" in which he contended a duel "involves the violation of my conscience and the hazard of my family, as against a man who has neither conscience nor family." Stephens and the Democratic Party ticket carried Georgia, but Hill established himself as a brilliant comer.

The following year, at the age of thirty-four, he became the American Party candidate for governor against Brown. But he lost the election due to the backlash of his own brilliance coupled with the relative unpopularity of the radical America First policies of the Know-Nothings.

Two years later he was elected to the State Senate where he became leader of the opponents to secession. As such, he also was elected to the State Convention in 1861 where he and Stephens found themselves uncomfortable allies in their unsuccessful fight to keep Georgia in the Union. There is no record of the speeches made before the Convention, but obviously Hill was at his oratorical best because his remarks so offended some of his friends that he was burned in effigy. Once the decision was made, however, he accepted it and was elected to the Provisional Congress of the Confederate States where he was a principal figure in drafting the Constitution and organizing the government.

Hill subsequently was elected to the Confederate Senate where he served throughout the Civil War as Jefferson Davis' staunchest and most vocal supporter and defender. While Bob Toombs, Stephens, and Brown were criticizing and hamstringing Davis and the Richmond government, Hill went on a speaking tour throughout the South, encouraging his fellow southerners to continue their efforts even after it was obvious that the cause was lost.

Davis later said Hill "stood by me when all others forsook our cause" and "proved himself the truest of the true." After Hill's death, Davis had an opportunity to repay him by leaving his sickbed to attend ceremonies dedicating Hill's statue in Atlanta. There he declared, "If I had to choose the three greatest Georgians, I would choose Oglethorpe the benevolent, Troup the dauntless, and Hill the faithful."

Hill was so loved by his slaves that, when he freed them at the end of the war, they refused to leave his service. Not one of them betrayed him or the former Confederate leaders who sought refuge from time to time in his home in LaGrange. He was arrested in May 1865 and imprisoned until July when he was paroled by President Andrew Johnson.

Hill resumed his law practice and lost $30,000 trying to prove cotton could be raised with free labor on his farms in Southwest Georgia. For three years he was an outspoken critic of the Reconstruction Acts of 1867. Realizing that further resistance was futile, however, he reversed himself and began to urge acceptance and compliance. Earlier he had strongly criticized Joe Brown for doing the same thing, but now found himself on the receiving end of public scorn.

By 1875, Hill's public image was sufficiently restored for him to be elected to the United States House of Representatives. In one fell swoop he achieved complete forgiveness from his fellow Georgians with his stormy triumph in the debate with Blaine who was trying to get the Republican presidential nomination by defaming Davis. Hill, in one of his finest oratorical moments, thundered from the floor of the House: "I tell you that this reckless misrepresentation of the South must stop right here. I put you upon notice that hereafter when you make any assertion against her, you must be prepared to substantiate it with proof."

It was also on the House floor that, in the course of delivering what is called his Amnesty Speech, he made the following, often-quoted declaration: "There is no more Confederacy! We are back in the House of our Fathers, our Brothers are our companions, and we are at home to stay, thank God!" An excerpt from this speech is carved on the base of his statue in the Georgia State Capitol.

There was no doubt from the moment of his ringing defense of Davis that he would be elected to the next vacancy in the United States Senate. This took place on January 26, 1877, and he served there with distinction and as a respected exponent of his original Unionist views until his death. His senior colleague was his former political enemy, Joe Brown, and the two of them patched up their long-standing differences, became close friends, and developed into one of the most effective senatorial teams in Congress.

But that great irony among the many ironies in his full and colorful life is perhaps outranked by those of his death which came slowly and painfully as the result of cancer of the tongue. Before his demise he was visited by a forgiving Alexander Hamilton Stephens who was moved to write of him in his final book then going to press: "One of the brightest lights went out. . . . He possessed oratorical gifts in an eminent degree. In power of statement and force of invective he had few if any superiors. His death was universally lamented."

James Jackson

(Lawyer, Patriot, Hero of American Revolution, General of Georgia Militia, Opponent of Yazoo Fraud, Congressman, twice Governor, twice United States Senator. Born September 21, 1757, Moreton-Hampstead, Devonshire, England. Died March 19, 1806, Washington, D. C.)

James Jackson was a short man with a short name and a short temper, but he stood tall in courage, honesty, and love of Georgia. He ranks among the greatest patriots and fighters of corruption in the nation's history. No one was certain exactly how short he was because he was so sensitive about the subject that his friends did not mention it and his enemies could not get close enough to measure him. His friends revered him, Thomas Spalding, referring to him as "the noblest man with whom it has been my lot to be acquainted." His enemies belittled him, Chief Justice Henry Osborne, for whose impeachment he was responsible, calling him a "brawling pigmy."

During the course of his brief, colorful life of forty-nine years he fought twenty-three duels. By his own admission in an autobiographical sketch, he was "the first boy . . . who bore arms" in the American Revolution. He was destined to be involved in both the first act of rebellion and the last armed engagement of that conflict in Georgia.

Jackson resigned his seat in the United States Senate to come home to fight and reverse the wholesale corruption of Georgia state government known as the Yazoo Fraud. He also wrote the new State Constitution to prevent any repetition of it and gave the state its historic seal with its classic arch and memorable motto chosen from Plato's **Republic,** "Wisdom, Justice and Moderation."

James came to Georgia at the age of fifteen under the

auspices of his father's friend, lawyer John Wereat, who later was to serve briefly as Georgia's third governor. Before his eighteenth birthday, Jackson joined Joseph Habersham and the Liberty Boys in raiding the King's Ammunition Stores and sending powder to New England for use in the Battle of Bunker Hill.

He was only nineteen when he participated in the burning of the British rice ships in Savannah harbor and was not yet twenty when he served as a Lieutenant under General James Screven (who was executed after his surrender). The young soldier was wounded in the ankle in the first encounter with British troops invading Georgia between Midway and Sunbury. He escaped when the British captured Savannah and, because of his British accent, was almost executed as a Tory spy when taken prisoner on his way to join General Moultrie in South Carolina.

Jackson took part in the Siege of Savannah by the French and Americans and was a particular favorite of Comte d'Estaing in what he called "the storm of Savannah," at which time he also came to the attention of General Nathaniel Greene. Greene said that, despite his dirty uniform and straw hat, there was "something in his countenance" that impressed him. It was Jackson who captured Major McArthur, the commander of the famous 71st Scotch Foot, in the Battle of Cowpens, and he also played a major role in the recapture of Augusta. He was made Commander of that garrison where he uncovered a plot for mutiny and his own murder. He had the personal satisfaction of supervising the courts-martial and hangings of the ringleaders.

In 1781 he was promoted to Lieutenant Colonel and made commander of the Georgia State Legion, a tatterdemalion outfit composed of two companies of cavalry and one of infantry. According to Jackson, the members were uniformed in "Deer Skin dressed and turned up with what little blue cloth I could procure" and were armed with pistols and swords which Jackson himself "turned out." They fought in and around Savannah, specializing in daring raids into Savannah to harass the British and capture horses and supplies. On one such foray, they even burned the barns of Royal Governor Wright. When the British evacuated Savannah, General Wayne accorded the 25-year-old Colonel Jackson the honor of accepting the keys to the city in consideration of his "severe and tedious services in the advance." Jackson and his men subsequently fought in the final skirmish of the Revolution in Georgia on Skidaway Island.

He served as Clerk of Court by election of the First and Second Provincial Congresses in 1776 and 1777 and as a member of the First Constitutional Convention of Georgia in 1777. Following the Revolution, he studied law. A grateful Georgia General Assembly made him a General in the State Militia, presented him title to the former home and land of Governor Wright known as "Cedar Hill," and elected him Governor in 1788. He declined the office, however, because he felt he was too young for the job. He was elected instead to the First Congress in 1789 and contested the election of General Wayne to the Second Congress. His oratory on this occasion earned him an ovation by Congress and castigation as a "damn liar" by Wayne. As a result, the seat was declared vacant and Chief Justice Osborne was impeached for his election machinations in Camden County.

Jackson then was elected to the United States Senate where he served from March 4, 1793, until he resigned in 1795 to return home to seek election to the General Assembly and to overturn the Yazoo Act. By this scheme legislators had enriched themselves in a sorry exercise of wholesale corruption by selling Georgia's western lands to speculators. This Jackson denounced as "a Confiscation Act of the rights of your Children & Mine, & unborn Generations, to supply the rapacious graspings of a few sharks." He crusaded against the legislation in letters to the newspapers which he signed "Silicus" (later published in a book, **The Letters of Silicus to the Citizens of Georgia**). In addition, he made speeches throughout the state telling the people how they had been robbed of their lands, declaring: "I and my comrades fought for them in the Revolution. They belong to you and your children. The legislature has no right to vote them away. This dreadful wrong must be righted."

Jackson carried the day in the General Assembly and, when Governor Jared Irwin signed the repeal, he and his colleagues carried the original act onto the grounds of the State Capitol at Louisville. Using a magnifying glass, they called "down fire from heaven to burn such vile papers." The spot where this dramatic action occurred is marked today with a stone on the lawn of the Jefferson County Courthouse. Ironically, the leader of the opposition to repeal was Jackson's former colleague in the United States Senate, General James Gunn, to whose seat Jackson was elected when his term expired in 1801. Jackson thus became the only man in Georgia history to serve in both the Few and Gunn lines of senatorial succession.

The General Assembly elected Jackson governor in 1798 and again in 1800. As Chief Executive, Jackson forbade any mention of the Yazoo Acts in Georgia's legal reports and fought three duels over the matter with Robert Watkins, the lawyer appointed to edit and publish the reports of the General Assembly. Watkins called Jackson "the leader of the damn venal set or faction who have disgraced their country." He was permanently crippled in the third duel by wounds which plagued him until his death. As he lay helpless on the dueling field, he cursed Watkins: "Damn it, Watkins, I thought I would give you another shot." But he did have the satisfaction of seeing retribution visited on those responsible for the scandal. Most were defeated, one was hanged, one moved to South Carolina and was murdered, some went into hiding from the scorn of their neighbors, and others were boycotted socially and in business.

It was during Jackson's tenure that the Constitution of 1798 was drafted. This document contained a provision to prevent similar legislative corruption which continues to this day, the requirement that all subject matters contained in bills must be set forth in their titles, thereby preventing secret enactments in the small print of lengthy acts. It was a Constitution which lasted Georgia with only twenty-three amendments until the Civil War.

He was elected a second time to the United States Senate in 1801 and served from March 4 of that year until his death on March 29, 1806, in Washington, D. C. His demise was announced to the Senate by his colleague Abraham Baldwin, an intimate friend of twenty years and former compatriot in the Revolution, who had been at his bedside as he "closed his eyes just at the dawning of the day." In eulogy, Baldwin told the Senate, "In sterling integrity and honest devotion to public duty, I have never found his superior." He would have been pleased with the inscription John Randolph of Virginia wrote for his simple tombstone in the Congressional Cemetery: "The scourge and terror of corruption at home."

Jackson never was honored in death as he was in life, the only monument to his memory being a tablet erected at the site of his residence in Savannah in 1949. On that occasion, the late Alexander A. Lawrence, then President of the Georgia Historical Society, thus decried that omission:

"We in Savannah have sadly failed our duty to this great Georgian. . . . Perhaps some day our obligation in that respect will be performed. It will not be until a monument is erected here comparable to those that honor Oglethorpe, Greene, Gordon, Pulaski or Jasper. More than that beneath this monument should be laid the ashes of General Jackson. His remains should be brought back from Washington to the State he loved. 'If after his death his heart could be opened, Georgia would be legibly read there,' he once observed. . . . For such a man eternal rest in the Washington of our day must be a fitful and troubled one."

The monument of which Jackson would have been proudest, however, was an intangible one — the election of both his son and grandson to the United States Congress.

Robert Tyre "Bobby" Jones, Jr.

(Engineer, Lawyer, Writer, World's Greatest Golfer, Only Winner of The Grand Slam, Founder of The Masters Tournament. Born March 17, 1902. Died December 18, 1971, Atlanta, Georgia.)

Incomparable is the only word which comes close to describing Bobby Jones, the greatest golfer the world ever has seen or ever is likely to see. Many writers have tried to assess Jones' significance and achievements, but the late Jim Townsend expressed it most aptly when he said:

"The essence of Bob Jones is that he was never ordinary.

"The premier athlete of our times, his records as a golfing champion stand today as remote and unapproachable as they have through the decades since he charmed the world with his flashing good looks and unrelenting brilliance on the golf course.

"No sports figure — not Ruth nor Dempsey nor Grange — so captured the imagination of the nation with his single-handed achievements as did Bobby Jones. He was a Lindbergh."

From the time he won the East Lake Junior Golf Championship in Atlanta in 1911 at the age of nine until he retired from the game in 1930 at the age of twenty-eight, Bobby Jones attracted the awe and admiration of everyone who had the privilege of seeing him follow through from the classic stance of his powerful swing to the deadeye accuracy of the putts made with his "Calamity Jane." Jones retired at the apex of his career, after winning what the late O. B. Keeler colorfully described as "the impregnable quadrilateral of golf" — The Grand Slam of the American and British Amateur and Open Golf Championships.

After winning the Georgia State Amateur Championship at

fourteen, he became a national figure the same year by qualifying for the U. S. National Amateur and making it into the quarterfinals before losing to the defending champion. It was that tournament, according to Keeler, in which Bobby learned the four lessons which carried him to unequaled greatness in fourteen years — self-control, resoluteness in coming from behind, and ignoring both the gallery and one's opponent to play only "against the iron certitude of par," traits which later caused some critics to accuse him unjustly of being "cold and aloof."

Jones gave exhibitions during World War I when no tournaments were held and played in twenty major championships without winning a single title over the course of seven years. He did all this while pursuing his academic studies. He was an excellent student and earned degrees in mechanical engineering from Georgia Tech and English Literature from Harvard. Then he broke into the winning column at the age of twenty-one with a magnificent, 184-yard, over-the-water shot from the rough to within six feet of the pin on the 18th hole of the playoff with Bobby Cruickshank for the 1923 U. S. Open Championship at Inwood Country Club, Long Island. That ended what Keeler called Bobby's "Seven Lean Years" and began his "Seven Fat Ones" in which all of his unequaled triumphs were achieved.

From 1923 through 1930 he won thirteen of the twenty-seven major tournaments in which he played — five U. S. Amateur, four U. S. Open, three British Open, and one British Amateur Titles. He was a national champion eight years in succession — U. S. Open in 1923, U. S. Amateur in 1924 and 1925, U. S. Open in 1926, U. S. Amateur in 1927 and 1928, U. S. Open in 1929, and U. S. Open and Amateur in 1930. In addition, he claimed the British Open Titles in 1926, 1927, and 1930 and the British Amateur Title in 1930.

Upon his return home after winning the British Amateur at St. Andrews and the British Open at Hoylake in 1930, he was given a ticker tape parade down Broadway in New York City which excelled that honoring Charles Lindbergh three years earlier. He went on to win the U. S. Open at Interlachen and the U.S. Amateur at Merion to complete the Slam. Even greater than the achievement of the Slam, Keeler believes, is the fact that in the last nine years of his career, Bobby played in twelve open championships, nine American and three British, and finished first or second in eleven of those twelve starts. It was Keeler's belief that, because of the nature of the game and the

120

fact that only an amateur can equal those feats, Jones' records never will be broken or seriously challenged.

Two years prior to achieving the Grand Slam, Bobby completed his law studies at Emory University, passed the bar examination, and joined his father's Atlanta law firm. It was his choice to pursue a legal career rather than turn professional. So, at the pinnacle of his achievement he retired from competitive golf, saying, "The Grand Slam seemed to leave nothing lacking. By keeping on I might add one or more championships to the total, but it seemed that even the most I could hope for would be an anticlimax. I knew I could never do another Grand Slam, nor would I ever try."

Golf remained his first love, however, and he wrote more than half a million words in three books and countless columns about the game. He also made a number of instructional films about golf and designed clubs for A. G. Spalding. But his crowning post-retirement achievement came when he joined in partnership with New York financier Clifford Roberts and the noted golf course designer, Dr. Alistair Mackenzie, to plan the Augusta National Golf Club and to establish the Masters Golf Tournament. Since 1934 the Masters has developed into an annual event rivaling the U. S. Open in prestige and financial rewards and has achieved recognition as the World Series of golf. Until his health failed, Jones personally extended the invitations to the Tournament and the only thing more coveted in the game today than one of the Club's invitations to participate is one of the green jackets signifying the winning of a Masters Championship.

Bobby's initial interest in golf was whetted because his frail health as a boy prompted his father to buy a house adjacent to the East Lake Golf Course where the child could enjoy and benefit from a life in the open. Bobby so took to the sport that he began following and with a stick imitating the swing and stance of Golf Pro Stewart Maiden. He so impressed an adult friend that he was given a cut-down cleek when he was five years old which inspired him and a playmate to lay out their own four-hole backyard course.

Ill health similarly marked Jones' last years. He was stricken in 1948 with the mysterious spinal disease syringomyelia which relentlessly ravaged and crippled his robust frame and reduced him to one cane, then two canes, and finally to a wheelchair. This after volunteering and serving with distinction as a Lieutenant Colonel in the Army during World War II. Openly acknowledging that death was the only cure, he fought back for twenty-three years with courage and fortitude which earned him even greater admiration than his feats on the links. Despite his illness, he continued to pursue his legal career, to write, and to make as many appearances as physically possible until he died of an aneurism in 1971.

By his own account, the most moving experience of his life came in 1958 when he made the painful trip back to St. Andrews, where he had triumphantly won the British Amateur Title in 1930, as Captain of the American Team in the First World Amateur Golf Team Championship. Now he became the first American since Benjamin Franklin and the eighth person in history to receive the Freedom of the City, the highest honor that birthplace of golf bestows. Unable to walk, Jones rode down the aisle of the auditorium in an electric golf cart, and the dramatic moment was described by Herbert Warren Wind in **Sports Illustrated** as follows:

"He said near the end of his talk, 'I could take out of my life everything except my experience at St. Andrews and I'd still have a rich, full life.'

"He left the stage and got into his electric golf cart. As he directed it down the center aisle to leave, the whole hall (1700 people) spontaneously burst into the old Scottish song, 'Will Ye No' Come Back Again?' So honestly heartfelt was this reunion for Bobby Jones and the people of St. Andrews (and for everyone) that it was ten minutes before many who attended were able to speak again with a tranquil voice."

In his later years Jones was friend and confidant of many of the great leaders of the nation and the world. He developed a particularly warm friendship with President Eisenhower. As a token of this friendship he had "Mamie's Cabin" built adjacent to the grounds of the Augusta National Golf Club. It was there that Ike, in gratitude, painted a handsome portrait of Bobby.

Bobby Jones was a man as modest and unassuming as he was talented and exceptional. Of his accomplishments, he said that he "learned what I know from defeats." When he was named a first-year inductee into the Georgia Athletic Hall of Fame in 1964, he said, "I modestly expected to be named to the National Golf Hall of Fame, but it never occurred I'd ever be in an athletic Hall of Fame. I never thought of myself as an athlete."

The late Ralph McGill summed him up in these words: "He is a man who never took himself or his feats seriously enough to stuff his shirt with them. Of them all, his feet are freest of clay, the man himself most devoid of guile, envy, false pride and overriding ambition."

122

Martin Luther King, Jr.

(Minister, Civil Rights Leader, Advocate of Nonviolent Social Change, Winner of Nobel Peace Prize. Born January 15, 1929, Atlanta, Georgia. Died April 4, 1968, Memphis, Tennessee. Entombed at Martin Luther King, Jr., Center for Social Change in Atlanta, Georgia.)

Few men in history have affected the lives of more people or exerted a more positive influence on the course of human events both in life and in death than Martin Luther King, Jr.

A black minister with an unequaled capacity for articulating the heartfelt aspirations of the downtrodden masses, Dr. King preached and practiced the love of one's fellowmen espoused by Jesus Christ and the doctrine of passive resistance perfected by Mohandas K. Gandhi. He succeeded not only in giving hope to oppressed people throughout the world but also in bringing his own country to make good the promises of equality for all upon which it was founded but to which it had given little more than lip service for almost two centuries.

His movement, coupled with the tragic assassination of President John F. Kennedy, shamed the American people into writing into law the rights they both claimed collectively and denied selectively on the basis of race, color, creed, sex, and other subjective factors. Through the Martin Luther King, Jr., Center for Social Change in Atlanta, his principles are being carried forward and translated into reality on an ever-broadening basis by his widow, Mrs. Coretta Scott King.

Of all the dramatic scenes which have unfolded across the panorama of civilized man's experience, few can compare with the moment in 1963 when Dr. King stood on the steps of the Lincoln Memorial in Washington, D. C., and enthralled what probably was the largest peaceful, voluntary assembly in history with his soaring oratory in which he painted a vivid word picture of the dream he had for mankind — " . . . a dream that one day this nation will rise up and live out the true meaning of its creed, 'We hold these truths to be self-evident, that all men are created equal' . . . that one day on the red hills of Georgia, sons of former slaves and the sons of former slave owners will be able to sit down together at the table of brotherhood . . . that my four little children will one day live in a nation where they will not be judged by the color of their skin, but by the content of their character." When he concluded with the words of the Negro spiritual which subsequently were engraved as the epitaph on his tomb, "Free at last, Free at last. Thank God Almighty, we are free at last!" there occurred one of history's electric moments thus described by Mrs. King in her book:

"As Martin ended, there was the awed silence that is the greatest tribute an orator can be paid. And then a tremendous crash of sound as two hundred and fifty thousand people shouted in ecstatic accord with his words. The feeling that they had of oneness and unity was complete. They kept on shouting in one thunderous voice, and for that brief moment the Kingdom of God seemed to have come on earth."

The son and grandson of Baptist ministers, Martin Luther King, Jr., was reared in the comfortable circumstances of the black middle class and had little personal experience with racial discrimination and social injustice during his youth, although his father always was outspoken on those subjects. He was a serious student who passed the entrance examination for Morehouse College at the age of fifteen. He received his divinity degree from Crozer Theological Seminary in Chester, Pennsylvania, where his interest in the precepts of Gandhi began. Later he received an earned Ph. D. Degree from Boston University at the same commencement at which Senator John F. Kennedy received an honorary one.

He became pastor of the Dexter Avenue Baptist Church in Montgomery, Alabama, two months before Mrs. Rosa Parks touched off the bus boycott when she refused to relinquish her seat to a white man. His lifelong identity with civil rights causes began when he was elected President of the Mont-gomery Improvement Association formed to lead the success-ful fight against Alabama's state and local bus segregation laws. It was during that fight that he enunciated the principle from which he never retreated, "We will not resort to violence. We will not degrade ourselves with hatred. Love will be returned for hate." He also experienced the first of many acts of violence directed against him and his family, a bomb being thrown onto the porch of his home with his wife, baby daughter, and a friend inside narrowly escaping injury.

In 1957, King and sixty black ministers from throughout the South organized the Southern Christian Leadership Conference, and, after a trip to India for further study of Gandhi's techniques of nonviolence, moved to Atlanta where he became co-pastor with his father of Ebenezer Baptist Church. Now he began to spend all his time crusading for civil rights for blacks.

He was arrested with students who staged a sit-in to desegregate the lunch counter at Rich's Department Store in Atlanta. While that trespass charge was dropped, he was sentenced to six months in Reidsville State Prison on an earlier charge of driving with an invalid Georgia license. The telephone call which Senator Kennedy made to Mrs. King while he was imprisoned is said to have been responsible for his election as President in the campaign then in progress. Soon thereafter he was arrested again in the demonstrations in Albany, Georgia, where officials opted to shut down all public parks and swimming pools rather than desegregate them.

Dr. King and his followers braved police dogs and fire hoses in their campaign to desegregate restaurants, hotels, and department stores in Birmingham, Alabama. While jailed there, he wrote his famous "Letter From Birmingham Jail" delineating his moral philosophy. That was followed by the March on Washington during which his memorable "I Have A Dream" speech was delivered and he and his associates had a White House meeting with President Kennedy. The following year he was jailed for leading demonstrations in St. Augustine, Florida, and stood beside President Lyndon Johnson when he signed the Civil Rights Act of 1964 which opened public accommodations to all citizens.

Perhaps the greatest single moment in his career occurred on December 10, 1964, when he became, at thirty-five, the youngest person ever to receive the Nobel Peace Prize. He accepted it as "a profound recognition that nonviolence is the answer to the crucial political and moral questions of our time — the need for man to overcome oppression without resorting to violence and oppression." A man not given to pretensions, he objected to wearing formal dress with striped trousers, tailcoat, and ascot to the presentation ceremonies held at Oslo University, and he vowed "never to wear one of these things again." And he did not.

After Hosea Williams and other assistants were beaten in the "Bloody Sunday" demonstration in Selma, Alabama, in 1965, he led 25,000 protesters on a Freedom March from Selma to Montgomery which culminated in the enactment of the 1965 Voting Rights Act.

The following year he enlarged his campaign against discrimination to include opposition to the Vietnam War, a stand for which he was more maligned and vilified than for his civil rights activities and which cost him his friendship with President Johnson. He also took his crusade to Chicago where he was stoned, and went to Birmingham to serve a jail term growing out of the 1963 demonstrations there when it was upheld by the United States Supreme Court. In November 1967 he announced plans for his Poor Peoples Campaign, but did not live to see it come to fruition.

King went to Memphis in 1968 to lead protests by striking garbage workers only to be gunned down by James Earl Ray on April 4 as he stood on the balcony of the Lorraine Motel. The shock of his death touched off rioting and violence in major cities, particularly Washington, D. C. His funeral in Atlanta was attended by tens of thousands of his followers who marched in a procession through Atlanta following the coffin carried on a farm wagon pulled by two humble mules, "Belle" and "Ada."

The Martin Luther King, Jr., Memorial Center was established in Atlanta on January 15, 1969, in observance of his fortieth birthday, and his body was removed to a permanent tomb on a memorial plaza adjacent to the Ebenezer Baptist Church and facing the Center across Auburn Avenue. The name of the Center was changed in 1972 to the Martin Luther King, Jr., Center for Social Change. Under the direction of his widow as President, it is moving steadily forward in the expansion of facilities and programs and enjoys international status in its work to combat discrimination in all its forms. At the same time it seeks improvement in the social and economic lot of poor, oppressed, and deprived people throughout the world. The Center is a major stop on the itinerary of virtually every foreign dignitary visiting the United States. Its mission was stated by Mrs. King upon the occasion of the name change in these words: "My husband was a man with a philosophy and a program. Our Center must lead in preserving that philosophy with a program — a program that aggressively challenges the injustices and violence he challenged."

When President Kennedy was assassinated, Dr. King

126

predicted to Mrs. King a similar fate for himself. But it was a prospect on which he did not dwell, having told her also that, "If you are cut down in a movement that is designed to have the soul of a nation, then no other death could be more redemptive." At the time of the Kennedy death, he issued a statement which is perhaps even more fitting in application to himself: "The posture of his life has written an epitaph that lives beyond the boundaries of death."

Sidney Clopton Lanier

(Lawyer, Teacher, Soldier, Poet, Author, Linguist, Mathematician, Musician, Lecturer. Born February 3, 1842, Macon, Georgia. Died September 7, 1881, in North Georgia Mountains.)

Although more than a century after his untimely death critics still debate the degree of his greatness and the breadth of his genius, none questions the ranking of Sidney Clopton Lanier as "The Poet of the South" or fails to marvel at the unique colorfulness of his short life's experiences. These experiences ran the gamut from Civil War blockade running to enthralling performance as a self-taught symphony orchestra flautist. No modern soap opera script could equal the drama or tragedy of the thirty-nine years and seven months of this frail, but daring and dynamic, southerner's true adventures.

The fact that men of letters seem unable to put him in a literary or academic niche does as much as any critical assessment to demonstrate that he was one of a kind rather than one of a school. His works are reminiscent of Milton and Ruskin, follow the paths of the New England Romantics Longfellow, Whittier, and Lowell, and were influenced by the styles of Tennyson and Swinburne. Yet they are totally individualistic in scenic imagery and profound mysticism such as characterize his classic verses in "The Song of the Chattahoochee" and "The Marshes of Glynn" which are beloved and endlessly discussed and recited the world over. He could be as lofty and inspiring as his contemporary Poe was terrifying and depressing and, though in his life he loved only one woman, his beautiful wife Mary, of his love poems it has been said "never has true conjugal love . . . been more truly sung." His biographer, A. H. Starke, summed him up as "a man who was far in advance of his times, a southerner who refused to be sectional and a champion of artistic and social experimentation in an age of stagnant conservatism."

Lanier's temperament and philosophy were reflections of the powerful and contradictory influences upon him as a precocious and impressionable youth growing up in antebellum Macon, Georgia. He was pampered by a doting grandfather who made, lost, and regained fortunes in the hotel business. It was his grandfather who early introduced Sidney to the luxuries and excitement of the Lanier House, Macon's leading hotel, which catered to travelers taking the stagecoach from New York to New Orleans and the steamboats plying the Ocmulgee River between Macon and Darien.

He was sternly disciplined by a bitter and frustrated father who spent an unhappy life, after dropping out of college to marry, trying to make a living as a self-taught lawyer and having to rely on the generosity of his rich father. Young Sidney was taught music, art, and the classics on the one hand and the harsh doctrine of predestination of the Presbyterian Church on the other by his aristocratic Virginia mother. And he amused himself by spending long hours observing nature in the Ocmulgee River swamps, teaching himself to play the flute so well he could fool birds with their own calls. He also enjoyed swapping musical knowledge with Negro barber John Booker who later was to travel the world with his own minstrel show. Lanier established his own minstrel troupe and trained his own military company among local youths in Macon, dreaming of turning the city into a great world art center like Athens. He also traded "corny" jokes and tried out his "doggerel" verse on his lifelong chum, Willie LeConte, nephew of the famed scientists and educators, Doctors John and Joseph LeConte.

Before his fifteenth birthday he passed the rigorous examination in Latin, Greek, and New Testament which admitted him to the sophomore class of Oglethorpe University, a Presbyterian School at Midway near the State Capitol, Milledgeville. There he excelled in declamation and debate and came under the influence of Dr. James Woodrow, a maternal uncle of Woodrow Wilson and probably the first Ph. D. ever to teach in a Georgia school. Dr. Woodrow later was censured for his belief in evolution and was acknowledged by Lanier to have been the "strongest and most valuable stimulus" of his youth.

His father heard that Sidney with his flute, Willie LeConte with his violin, and John Lamar with his violoncello had formed a small orchestra and were gaining quite a reputation for serenading the young ladies of Midway and the politicians of Milledgeville. Fearing that Sidney might make music his life's career, Lanier's father forced him to leave school and take a job in the post office in Macon. But he saved his money and returned and was graduated with first honors on July 18, 1860, planning a career in teaching after being named a tutor in math at Oglethorpe.

Sidney was present at the State Capitol when Georgia seceded from the Union on January 19, 1861. In June he joined the Macon Volunteers of the Second Georgia Battalion with which he served through the campaign of 1862 in Virginia, having been joined by his adored and adoring younger brother, Cliff, shortly before the Battle of Drury Bluff.

The brothers saw war at its worst in the seven days of fighting around Richmond June 26-July 2, 1862, and later at Malvern Hill and Petersburg. Sidney refused a commission to keep from being separated from his brother, and both were transferred to the Mounted Signal Service in 1863 only to be separated the following year and assigned as signal officers on separate blockade runners. Sidney's ship was captured in November of that year, and he was sent to a worsening succession of federal prisons, culminating in three months at Point Lookout, Maryland. The torturous conditions there resulted in his contracting tuberculosis. He was released in February 1865 and walked home to Macon where he arrived more dead than alive.

The next eight years were marked by many tragedies, beginning with the death of his mother from tuberculosis in 1865. His own hemorrhage of the lungs forced him to give up teaching in 1868 and to take up the study and practice of law with his father. He married in 1867 after publishing his first and only novel, **Tiger Lilies,** which, though dismissed by critics as amateurish and superficial, was a powerful denunciation of war and violence. In search of a beneficial climate in 1872 he went to San Antonio, Texas, where acclaim for his flute concerts inspired him to return to Georgia determined to devote his life to music and poetry.

Setting out for New York City with his pen and flute, he stopped off in Baltimore where he auditioned for the renowned Asger Hamerik, director of the Peabody Conservatory of Music. His rendition of Hamerik's own "Blackbirds" was so brilliant that he was offered a position as first flautist with the Peabody Symphony Orchestra. He never made it to New York but settled in Baltimore to begin the brief, but prolific, performing and writing career which burned as bright and fast as a candle in a draft for the remaining eight years of his life.

Lanier contributed poems and articles to magazines and

contracted with a railroad to write a tourism book on Florida. His epic poem, "Corn," published in **Lippincott's Magazine** in 1875 brought him his first general attention as a poet, and it was followed by the highly-praised cantata, "The Symphony," which he wrote on recommendation of Bayard Taylor for the opening of the Centennial Exposition in Philadelphia in 1876. Those two works with the addition of "Psalm of the West" and a number of shorter verses constituted his first published volume of poetry in the fall of 1876.

In the winter of 1876-77 he gave a series of lectures on English Literature which led to his appointment as a Lecturer in English Literature at Johns Hopkins University. For the first time he had a decent salary for the support of his family. Those initial lectures were published after his death as **Shakespeare and His Forerunners.** The Johns Hopkins lectures became two books — **The Science of English Verse** (1879) and **The English Novel** published posthumously in 1883.

It was during this period that he was doing two kinds of writing — the poetry which was his first love and into which he poured his very soul and the edited volumes of other's works for young men. Among the latter which he admitted he did for the money, were **The Boy's Froissart** (1879), **The Boy's King Arthur** (1880), **The Boy's Mabinogion** (1881), and **The Boy's Percy** (published in 1882 after his death). Among the poems of this period were the greats like "The Song of the Chattahoochee," "The Marshes of Glynn," "The Crystal," "Individuality," "Own Against Robin," and the moving "Sunrise" which he dictated to Mary after he became too weak to hold a pen.

In the spring of 1881 he and his family made a desperate pilgrimage to the mountains of North Carolina to seek relief for his failing lungs. He died in Mary's arms not long after dictating this fitting verse:
"I was the earliest bird awake,
It was a while before dawn, I believe,
But somehow I saw round the world,
And the eastern mountaintop did not hinder me.
And I knew the dawn, by my heart, not by mine eyes."
Even more fitting was the Twentieth Century tribute that came when his name was given to the world's largest man-made lake impounded from the waters of the river immortalized by his verse, the Chattahoochee.

Crawford Williamson Long

(Physician, Surgeon, Pharmacist, Discoverer of Anesthesia. Born November 1, 1815, Danielsville, Georgia. Died June 16, 1878, Athens, Georgia.)

Dr. Crawford Williamson Long was a brilliant surgeon who chose to be a country doctor instead of a big city physician because of his strong desire to serve his fellowman. His unassuming humanitarianism almost cost him credit for the most beneficial achievement of medical history. His discovery that ether could be used as anesthesia banished fear and torture from the operating room and made possible all the surgical breakthroughs which characterize modern medicine.

Although both Connecticut and Massachusetts claim that ether was first used as anesthesia in their state, those claims have been discredited by incontrovertible documentation that Dr. Long's successful use of ether to perform painless surgery on March 30, 1842, predates the closest other claim by two years and eight months. Dr. Long has been enshrined in the National Hall of Fame in Washington, D. C., and the Anesthetists' Hall of the Royal Society of Medicine in London as the true discoverer of ether anesthesia.

Long, the son of an educator, was graduated second in his class at the University of Georgia where his roommate was Alexander Hamilton Stephens, later to be Vice President of the Confederacy and the second of two Georgians in the Hall of Fame. After teaching for a year, Long began the study of medicine first under a preceptor and then at Transylvania University. Finally he attended the University of Pennsylvania from which he received his degree in 1839.

For eighteen months Long worked in hospitals in New York City where he gained the reputation of being a skilled surgeon. But he forsook the potential rewards of a permanent practice there to locate in Jefferson, Georgia, a hamlet of less than 500 residents. He felt he best could satisfy his personal ambition to be of the most service to humanity in the smaller locale.

While in New York, Long had been impressed by the pain experienced by women in childbirth. For this reason he had resolved to try to find some means of alleviating their suffering. He found that means almost by accident. Long was asked by some young friends to provide them with some nitrous oxide, the so-called "laughing gas" used by traveling showmen of that day, for a party they were planning. Since he was unable to produce any in Jefferson, he suggested the use of sulphuric ether instead.

"I informed them . . . that I had a medicine (sulphuric ether) which would produce equally exhilarating effects; that I had inhaled it myself and considered it safe as the nitrous oxide gas," he wrote subsequently in **The Southern Medical and Surgical Journal.**

Invited to the party himself, Long observed that persons who inhaled the gas for amusement were impervious to the pain of barked shins and sprained ankles sustained in falls. From this he deduced that inhalation of a sufficient quantity of ether should produce insensitivity to the pains of childbirth.

But his first opportunity to test his theory came not in a case of childbirth but in that of a man, James Venable, who came to him for removal of a cystic tumor from his neck. Venable agreed to the experiment and, in the presence of four witnesses, one of whom was a well-known local physician, Dr. Long at the age of twenty-six performed the first operation made under ether anesthesia. He extirpated the tumor, and the patient later swore in an affidavit that he felt no pain during the surgery. The other witnesses gave similar sworn statements, all of the originals of which now are in the National Museum in Washington, D. C.

Dr. Long subsequently performed seven other operations in which he administered ether prior to September 30, 1846, when Dr. W. T. G. Morton of Boston gave ether to a Mr. Frost and extracted a tooth without pain.

Although Dr. Long did not seek a patent on his discovery or even publish his findings until the article he wrote for **The Southern Medical and Surgical Journal** in 1849, he made no secret of his discovery. To the contrary, he gave it the widest dissemination possible at that time among his fellow practitioners in the Jefferson area. Of course, there was no hospital in or near Jefferson where he could give a public demonstration of the procedure.

The issue as to the primacy of discovery of the anesthetic qualities of ether was joined in the fall of 1846 when Dr. Morton and his partner, Dr. Charles T. Jackson, who had recommended the use of ether to him, applied for a patent on what they called "letheon" (which was nothing more than sulphuric ether disguised by aromatic oils). The doctors went before the surgeons of the Massachusetts Hospital of Surgery and recommended a test of their new agent in an actual major operation. Doctors Bigelow, Haygood and Warren used it on October 16 in removing a tumor from a young man without pain. Eleven days later Doctors Jackson and Morton executed a sworn affidavit declaring themselves to be "the original and first inventors" of anesthetic ether. Dr. Bigelow published details of the operation in **The Medical Examiner** for December 1846, but referred to the substance used as "letheon" rather than ether. The operating amphitheater used for that surgery has been preserved as a memorial to Dr. Morton, and October 16 is observed as Ether Day in Boston.

Further complicating the controversy was the claim of Horace Wells of Connecticut that he had had one of his own teeth extracted without pain in 1844 after subjecting himself to the effect of nitrous oxide gas as an anesthetic. The State of Connecticut subsequently erected a monument to him in Hartford inscribed, "Horace Wells, who discovered anesthesia Nov. 2, 1844."

Doctors Jackson and Morton had a falling out in 1847 over their respective claims as to which was the originator of the idea of using ether as an anesthetic. Dr. Jackson contested the memorial Morton presented to Congress in 1854, asking that he be recognized as the discoverer of anesthesia and that the federal government pay him for the use of ether. Friends of Long and Wells also challenged the contention, although Long did not ask for any compensation. During this period, Dr. Jackson journeyed to Georgia to talk with Dr. Long and his witnesses and offered to recognize Dr. Long as the first to use ether if Dr. Long would recognize him as the originator of the idea. Dr. Long declined to do so and disputed Dr. Jackson's contention that he had the advantage of the priority of publication.

Dr. J. Marion Sims of New York treated on this point in an article in **The Virginia Medical Monthly** in 1877 as follows:

"It is true Dr. Long may not have published his discovery in he medical journals of the country, nor does it appear that the other claimants did; but exhibiting their experiments in the

134

large cities of New York and Boston, of course better facilities were offered for disseminating the facts throughout the medical world. However, abundant evidence has been produced by Dr. Long to prove that he made no secret of his discovery, but, on the contrary, communicated it as rapidly to the medical fraternity as his restricted and limited facilities would permit, and the fact that he did not publish it through the medical journals makes him none the less the true discoverer."

Senator William C. Dawson of Georgia led the successful fight to discredit the claims of Jackson, Morton, and Wells and their supporters in the Congress. Dr. Long made no active defense of himself, saying he simply stood upon the facts of the matter. Neither did he make any claim for an appropriation from Congress, stating that the only reward he ever wished was to be considered a "benefactor to mankind."

In 1850 Dr. Long purchased a lot at which is now the intersection of Peachtree, Broad, and Luckie Streets in the new city of Atlanta and built a brick home on that site. He moved from Jefferson to Atlanta because he believed Atlanta, with its four railroads, was destined to become a major population center. But he quickly found the young city too wide open and rowdy for his sedate tastes and in 1855 sold his property and moved to Athens. He felt he could give his growing family better educational advantages there as well as enjoy a more attractive social and cultural environment.

He lived and conducted a large and prosperous surgical practice in Athens until he died June 16, 1878, at the age of sixty-three. During the Civil War he headed a military hospital established on the campus of the University of Georgia and was decorated with the Southern Cross of Honor for that distinguished service. His simple grave in historic Oconee Hill Cemetery overlooks the scenic Oconee River. Of his resting place, his biographer, Dr. Joseph Jacobs, wrote:

"On my last visit to my old home in Athens, Georgia, I stood at the grave of this good and great man. On the bank of the beautiful Oconee River, in our Southland, with no monument of imposing grandeur, his resting place marked along with the simple marbles within the power of loved ones to place there, is the grave of the great discoverer; and the flowers that bloom in sweet profusion on the earth above him seemed to betoken the lofty sentiment I have heard him so often express, that he wished no recompense or reward for the priceless boon he had conferred on humanity, save the recognition that he had 'been a benefactor to mankind.' "

135

Few monuments have been erected to the memory of this giant of medicine who ranks in history with Jenner, Pasteur, and Lister. A marble shaft was erected in Jefferson, the University of Pennsylvania unveiled a medallion to his memory, and one of Atlanta's major hospitals bears his name. His bust is in Statuary Hall in the United States Capitol, his portrait is in the Georgia Capitol, and a marker was placed in his honor on the campus of the University of Georgia. There have been suggestions that a suitable memorial be erected at the point in downtown Atlanta where Peachtree, Broad, and Luckie Streets merge, but they have never come to more than discussed ideas.

Juliette Magill Kinzie "Daisy" Gordon Low

(Sculptress, Artist, Socialite, World Traveler, Founder of the Girl Scouts of the United States of America. Born October 31, 1860. Died January 18, 1927, Savannah, Georgia.)

Juliette Magill Kinzie Gordon Low preferred to be known as "Daisy." But by any name she was a blithe spirit who charmed great people from Queen Victoria to General William Tecumseh Sherman to Rudyard Kipling to First Ladies Wilson, Coolidge, and Hoover.

She was a first-rate sculptress and artist in her own right, introduced grits and other southern delicacies to British society at the turn of the century, and left an indelible mark on the women of Twentieth Century America by founding the Girl Scouts of the United States of America (they insist upon the full name instead of the abbreviated G. S. A.). She was a colorful and unpredictable character who believed women should live full lives and be self-sufficient and, through the movement she established, proceeded to see that they learned how to do such things as stop runaway horses and overpower and tie up burglars.

Her unconventional approach to life was a legacy from her irrepressible Chicago mother, Nellie Kinzie, who met her father, William Washington Gordon of Savannah, by sliding down the banisters of the Yale Library into his arms. Their marriage was a great pre-Civil War social event of the City of Savannah. At the outbreak of the Civil War, Mrs. Gordon chose to stay in the South with her husband, who became a Captain in the Confederate Army.

Born in 1860, Daisy and her older sister, Eleanor, grew up with the hardships and malnutrition which were the lot of

137

most southern families as the war lengthened and worsened. She remembered hiding the family silver from the Yankees and of General Sherman paying personal visits to the stately Gordon mansion to deliver letters from Mrs. Gordon's Chicago kin. Sherman spared the Gordon home from the torch and it has been preserved as a memorial to Mrs. Low. Young Daisy remembered getting her first taste of sugar sitting on the General's lap and of telling his companion, General Howard who had lost an arm in the conflict, "Well, I shouldn't wonder if my papa did it. He has shot lots of Yankees!"

Captain Gordon managed to restore the family fortunes within a reasonable time after the war, and Daisy was sent off to a series of fashionable private schools. She attended Stuart Hall and Edge Hill in Virginia and Mesdemoiselles Charbonniers in New York City, where her energy and idiosyncracies kept her in hot water and resulted in her writing home, "Mama, I can't keep all the rules, I'm too much like you."

After graduation she began a round of travels which carried her all over the United States and throughout much of the world. Eventually she went to Great Britain where in 1882 she met and fell in love with the wealthy English playboy, big-game hunter, and companion and confidant of the Prince of Wales, William Mackay Low who was known as "Willy." At first shocked because he represented everything the Gordon family abhorred, Daisy's parents acquiesced and accepted Willy and, on the anniversary date of her parents, they were married in a magnificent wedding in Savannah's Christ Church on December 21, 1886.

Although an accident on her honeymoon left her almost totally deaf, the bride plunged into the social life of the British Empire with the same verve and savoir faire which had characterized all of her earlier activities. She became a popular figure in the life of riding to the hounds, going to the races at Ascot and Newmarket, big-game hunting in Africa, and giving and attending endless houseparties, dinners and elaborate balls which formed the world of her husband.

Willy Low bought "Wellesbourne House" in the center of Warwickshire for Daisy, and it was there that she introduced the elite of London society to the delights of grits, ham, sweet potatoes, green corn, cucumber pickles, and other favorites of the Old South. It was also here she, after taking lessons from a blacksmith, single-handedly fashioned the wrought iron gates for the estate's entrance and personally carved a mantelpiece for the smoking room.

She set new fashion trends with her stunning Paris originals and wore diamonds and ostrich plumes when the Prince of Wales presented her to Queen Victoria at the Court of St. James and waltzed with her afterwards. These events gave the royal seal of approval to her acceptance into British society. Among the many stories told of her adventures and exploits are two favorites. Once she accompanied her friend, Rudyard Kipling, fishing while wearing a $1,500 evening gown designed for her by a famous French couturier. On another occasion she engaged in a spirited verbal conflict with a young journalist named Winston Churchill about some articles he had written disparaging some of her friends.

Willy's wanderings and romantic escapades resulted in separation after the turn of the century, but he died in 1905 before there was a divorce. There followed another round of travels until in 1911 she settled down in Paris to study sculpting and seriously develop her artistic talents. She had the good fortune there to meet and become closely acquainted with the man who was to give purpose to her life, General Sir Robert Baden-Powell, the organizer of Boy Scouts. After stimulating her interest in the programs of the Girl Guides which had been founded by his sister, Agnes, he urged her to organize a group of Girl Guides in a picturesque valley in Scotland. Her success was so satisfying that she decided introduce a similar program in America. She returned to Savannah and on March 12, 1912, organized the first Girl Guide troop in the United States.

The idea spread rapidly over the nation and gradually evolved into the "Girl Scouts" under the impetus of Daisy's promotional travels throughout the country. Among those whose interest she attracted and whose help she enlisted were Mrs. Woodrow Wilson; Mrs. Thomas A. Edison; Mrs. Corinne Robinson, the sister of Theodore Roosevelt; and later on both Mrs. Calvin Coolidge and Mrs. Herbert Hoover. In 1915, her dreams became a reality with the incorporation of the Girl Scouts of the United States of America in the District of Columbia, the adoption of a constitution and by-laws, and the establishment of a National Council.

From that time until the day of her death from cancer, she devoted her total effort to developing the organization, at one time even selling her pearls when finances ran low. She wrote the first Girl Scout Handbook, picked out the site of Camp Juliette Low on Lookout Mountain, and took great delight in telling ghost stories around the campfires there. She especially liked to tell the one about her grandmother who was kidnapped by Indians and named by them "Little Ship-Under-Full-Sail," an appellation also applied to Daisy in her peripatetic days as a traveling youth. She particularly thrilled to the girls singing to her the song they had written to the tune of "Dixie":

"Away down South in old Savannah,
First was raised the Girl Scout banner,
Daisy Low, Daisy Low, Daisy Low,
Founder dear.
Now Scouting spreads to either ocean,
Thousands bring you deep devotion
Daisy Low, Daisy Low, Daisy Low,
Founder dear!"

Before her death she had the satisfaction of seeing the initial development of an international organization and of seeing the establishment at the British Girl Scout Camp of a cottage called "The Link." The building was set aside for members from all nations and dedicated to her and her "worldwide family of scouts and guides."

Her greatest regret in life was that she never had children of her own, but she is loved and revered by a family of present and former Girl Scouts which now numbers into the millions. Her birthplace in Savannah is a popular attraction for tourists from throughout the world.

Juliette Gordon Low's life and works have been honored by the issuance of a commemorative stamp and the naming of a Liberty Ship for her during World War II. But she is most remembered for her spirit, vitality, and zest for life which live to inspire modern women to be all they can be.

One of her friends summed it up well when she commented on the occasion of the dedication of her Savannah memorial: "The world is a much duller place now that Daisy has left it."

Ralph Emerson McGill

(Journalist, Syndicated Columnist, Author, World Traveler, Sports Editor, Executive Editor, Editor and Publisher of **The Atlanta Constitution,** *Winner of Pulitzer Prize. Born February 5, 1898, Soddy, Tennessee. Died February 3, 1969, Atlanta, Georgia.)*

Enlightened Southerners and liberals everywhere considered Ralph McGill to be the reincarnation of Henry W. Grady and called him the "Conscience of the South." On the other hand, racist politicians and their followers regarded him as no less than Satan incarnate, referring to him as "Rastus McGill" and by other names unprintably worse.

But by whatever frame of reference, his daily column printed down the left side of the front page of **The Atlanta Constitution** was universally read and thoroughly discussed or cussed, depending upon the points of view of individual readers. For more than three decades he probably had more influence on public action and reaction in the South than any other journalist or politician.

In his later years that influence extended far beyond his beloved Southland. Throughout all the Free World, which he traveled with regularity, he was respected and received by leaders who sought his views and advice. He received the highest honor which can come to a journalist, the Pulitzer Prize, along with virtually every other major recognition a writer can receive. Included were seventeen honorary doctorates from such outstanding institutions of higher learning as Harvard, Columbia, Notre Dame, and Emory Universities. Reporters and writers who had the privilege of working under him and with him stood in awe of his ability to sit down at a typewriter, with or without notes, and turn out his story or column without pause or the necessity of editing, revising, or rewriting any part of the finished copy.

Born in Tennessee, he worked his way through Vanderbilt University as a police and political reporter for **The Nashville Banner,** with time out to serve as a Marine in World War I. But he made his initial journalistic mark as a colorful sportswriter whose way with words made him Sports Editor of **The Banner** by the age of twenty-five and brought him to Atlanta and the same position on the **Constitution** shortly after he turned thirty.

For almost forty years he wrote a daily column, and his talent quickly proved too large to be confined to the athletic fields and sports reporting. In 1937 he was awarded a Rosenwald Fellowship to study farming and farm cooperatives in Scandinavia, Germany, France, and England. Thus he was on hand to report Hitler's invasion of Austria. In 1938 he was made Executive Editor, in 1942 he became Editor, and in 1960 he was elevated to Publisher which position he held at the time of his death nine years later from a sudden heart attack.

During the course of his career he served on the Committee of the American Society of Newspaper Editors which made a round-the-world trip in 1945 to talk with world leaders on developing a "free flow of information vital to post-war understanding." He covered the United Nations charter meeting in San Francisco and the Nuremburg Trials. Twice he visited Russia, including the trip made in 1959 with Vice President Nixon when the latter held his famous "kitchen" debate with Nikita Khrushchev. He visited West Africa on a six-week assignment for the U. S. Department of State. And he covered all the major presidential conventions and campaigns as well as Georgia politics during his years at the **Constitution.** His particular interest was young people, their education and their future, and he always made time in his schedule to see and talk with both American and foreign students.

McGill was perhaps the most prolific columnist of Twentieth Century American journalism, and never missed a deadline turning in his daily copy. In these columns he touched on everything from dogs to politics and farming to philosophy. One of his pet subjects to which he returned often was his continuing crusade against, in his words, "bad cooking generally and, especially, fraudulent southern cooking." Nothing aroused his Irish dander more than "Bar-B-Q" and Brunswick stew as they were usually served.

"Bar-B-Q," he wrote, "is almost invariably, half-done pork, cooked in some poor oven, and served well drenched with a hot sauce to hide the fact it is vile stuff." He abhorred Brunswick stew served up as "a slopping plate of coarse canned corn and tomatoes boiled with a handful of hamburger meat." He contended no real southerner would eat barbecue he did not see cooked and only then if it were "real barbecue" which would "practically melt in the mouth" after having been cooked at least twenty-four and preferably thirty-six hours over live, hickory coals. As for Brunswick stew, he described it in its true form as "a noble dish, being made of fat, contented hens, sweet young corn, tomatoes, much good butter, and tender cuts of fresh pork."

But the columns which attracted the greatest attention and comment and elicited the strongest reactions, both pro and con, were those he wrote about segregation, discrimination, civil rights, and the plight of black citizens caught in a dead-end society which relegated them to marginal and hopeless lives. He applauded the Supreme Court decision on school segregation and civil rights legislation and decried the bigotry of politicians and the hypocrisy of ministers who advocated defiance and preached hatred.

His Pulitzer Prize came in 1959 for his column of October 13, 1958, "A Church, a School — ," in which he lamented the attitudes and forces which had resulted in the bombing of Atlanta's Jewish Temple. He laid the blame for the wasting of that house of worship on the "rabid, mad-dog minds" responsible for the earlier bombing of the high school in Clinton, Tennessee, "the extremists of the citizens' councils" and "those so-called Christian ministers who have chosen to preach hate instead of compassion." He pointed out that "when the wolves of hate are loosed on one people, then no one is safe" and counseled that, while "it is late . . . there is time" for all Americans "to stand up and be counted on the side of law and the due process of law — even when to do so goes against personal beliefs and emotions." That and similar columns caused him to be the target of what the **Constitution** in a front page editorial the day after his death called "poisonous mail . . . incredible to decent men and women" and made his house the target of shotgun blasts and required special protection for his terminally-ill first wife during her final days.

Four volumes of his columns were compiled into books of which his favorite was **The Fleas Come With The Dog,** the title for which came from his Uncle Cade Worley in talking about the state of the nation. The book was a compilation of columns through which McGill attempted to show that, despite

143

the fact that the nation has "picked up a few fleas . . . a basic sense of values and a certain sense of humor can set us straight back on the road to freedom and dignity that we started out to travel."

In 1963 his fifth book, **The South and The Southerner** won **Atlantic Monthly's** Nonfiction Award and was translated into Japanese and published in Tokyo. In addition to his nationally syndicated columns and his books, McGill also found time to be a regular contributor of major articles to such publications as **Atlantic Monthly, Harpers, The New Republic, Saturday Evening Post, Reader's Digest, The New York Times Magazine,** and **The Reporter.** His papers have been preserved in the Special Collection section of the Woodruff Library for Advanced Studies at Emory University, including letters he received from the first Presidents he knew, Roosevelt, Eisenhower, Kennedy, Johnson, and Nixon.

Of all the tributes to his life and works, he undoubtedly would be proudest of the establishment in his memory of The McGill Scholarships given annually by Atlanta Newspapers, Inc., to promising and deserving young college journalism students. His memory also is honored annually by the Ralph McGill Lecture which brings an outstanding journalist to the campus of the University of Georgia under sponsorship of the Henry W. Grady School of Journalism and Mass Communication.

The impact of his writings and efforts to stamp out intolerance and bigotry was perhaps best summarized on the occasion of his death by Dr. Albert M. David of the Atlanta Chapter of the National Association for the Advancement of Colored People when he said:

"He interpreted the voice of all people who suffered, not only Negroes, but all people who wanted freedom. He was the only voice we had for 25 years. If anyone brought the South back into the Union it was Mr. McGill. We call Martin Luther King, Jr., a prophet, but McGill was a greater one because he didn't have to be."

Margaret Munnerlyn "Peggy" Mitchell Marsh

(Reporter, Writer, Author of **Gone With The Wind,** *Winner of Pulitzer Prize. Born November 8, 1900. Died August 16, 1949, Atlanta, Georgia.)*

Peggy Mitchell was a petite lady who stood only four feet eleven inches in her stocking feet and probably never weighed more than 100 pounds, but she produced a giant of a book which was larger than life from the date of its publication, a book which continues to have a life of its own in print and in film more than three decades after her death.

Only the Bible is a better seller than **Gone With The Wind,** and somewhere in the world at any given time some audience is reliving the glory and the agony of the Old and Reconstructed South as portrayed by the cinema greats Clark Gable, Vivien Leigh, Leslie Howard, and Olivia de Havilland. All but Miss de Havilland are deceased as is the creator of their characters and the chronicler of their travails in one of the most tragic eras of civilization.

Like virtually every other reporter and writer who ever put a word to paper, Peggy Mitchell, too, aspired to write "The Great American Novel." The story of how she almost did not is as enthralling and dramatic as were the vicissitudes of her heroine, Scarlett O'Hara.

It all happened because an ankle injury complicated by arthritis put her in a cast and on crutches and brought an end to her brief, but brilliant, career as a writer for **The Atlanta Journal Magazine.** Over a period of less than four years, she wrote for the magazine 129 full-length articles totaling more than 300,000 words. Her subjects were varied and often sensational, from a near-swooning interview with Rudolph Valentino to personally testing on the outside of a downtown

145

Atlanta skyscraper the apparatus sculptors would use in their work on the face of Stone Mountain.

She drove her second husband, utility advertising executive John R. Marsh, to distraction trying to keep pace with her voracious appetite for books, magazines, and other reading matter. It was his suggestion that she use the time on her hands to write a book, and he encouraged and helped her in doing so over a period of almost ten years between its start and publication.

After four years of work she had their Piedmont Road apartment literally awash with page after page of original, rewritten, and revised manuscript. She threw nothing away. Some of the envelopes which she used as files for each completed chapter were even used as doorstops. Working and revision were interspersed with trips throughout the Atlanta area, and particularly into Clayton County, the principal locale of the book.

She meticulously checked historical, genealogical, and tax records and cemetery tombstones to satisfy her obsession for historical accuracy, although she did not use the names of any real persons who lived then or since in that area. The author even had to find a substitute name for her heroine because of that determination.

Although she claimed she had no first chapter, she actually had done sixty or seventy versions, none satisfying her penchant for perfection. (In published format her original fifth chapter actually became the first.) Except for a title and the elusive first chapter, most of the work was done by 1930, and she spent the next five years in desultory editing and revising, scribbling rough notes and ideas on the outside of the chapter envelopes. But she never did reach the point where she thought it was ready for submission to potential publishers until one day in 1935 her friend and fellow writer, Medora Field Perkerson, wife of Angus Perkerson, Editor of **The Atlanta Journal Magazine,** invited her to have lunch with her and Harry Latham of The Macmillan Company.

At first Peggy refused to discuss her manuscript with Latham but, after much soul-searching and with John's encouragement, she called him at his hotel as he was preparing to leave town and offered to let him read her creation. He had to purchase a large suitcase to transport the big stack of dirty, dog-eared envelopes she delivered to him. He read the manuscript on his way to California and described it immediately as "the literary discovery of the year," a characterization he later revised to "century."

After the contract was signed, editing and rewriting began. Although there were many suggestions from John, Latham, and others, John later insisted that "every word in the book of 1037 pages is Peggy's own writing." Also, after much agonizing and many rejections, Peggy finally settled on a title from "Cynara," the poem by Ernest Dowson: "I have forgot much, cynara — gone with the wind." The completed manuscript was in the hands of the publisher in January 1936, was off the press June 30, 1936. In four months more than 700,000 copies had been sold.

J. Donald Adams, critic for the **New York Times Book Review,** called **Gone With The Wind** "beyond doubt one of the most remarkable first novels by an American writer," a fact supported by its winning the 1936 Pulitzer Prize and the National Book Award for the "Most Outstanding Novel." It was the Book-of-the-Month Club selection for July 1936 and won for Peggy the Carl Bohnenberger Award presented by the Southeastern Library Association in 1938 for "the most outstanding contribution to Southern literature during the last two years." It also won the Medal of Distinction from the New York Southern Society for the "most outstanding achievement in the perpetuation of tradition, history and customs of that part of the country."

The book was translated into twenty-one foreign languages and printed in Braille. David O. Selznick paid $50,000 for filming rights which, in those Depression days, was a fabulous sum. Peggy refused to have any role in the making of the movie which won ten Academy Awards. She left that to her fellow Georgia writer, Susan Myrick of Macon, although she is said to have wanted Basil Rathbone rather than Clark Gable to play the role of Rhett Butler. She was, Gable to the contrary notwithstanding, the star of the gala premier held in Atlanta December 13-15, 1939, the parade attracting people six deep on the streets from Hapeville to downtown Atlanta in an outpouring probably unequaled in Atlanta's history since the city's burning depicted in the novel.

Success and acclaim made little change in the modest lifestyle of Peggy and John Marsh, her only concession being to hire a secretary to help her personally answer thousands of letters and communications. Because she stayed out of the limelight, devoted her time to nursing John back to health following his heart attack, and refused to give interviews to any reporters other than Mrs. Perkerson, she was criticized for being shy and aloof. This description was strongly denied by her brother Stephen, who said, "She was not shy. She wanted to go on living just as she had been living. When strangers tried to get her to do things she did not want to do, she did not do them."

During World War II, as she had as a student during World War I, she served voluntarily as a Red Cross worker, participant in Bond-Selling Campaigns, and air raid warden for her block. She christened both the third and fourth cruisers to bear the name **USS Atlanta** and became a great favorite of prisoners at the Atlanta Federal Penitentiary. She went to the facility to receive their contributions from earnings in the prison shops and to tell them stories of how Georgia prisoners were released to fight for the Confederacy during the Civil War. (At her final rites, a wreath of flowers grown by those inmates was one of only two floral offerings accepted, the other being a massive blanket of snow-white flowers presented by the florists of Atlanta.)

Peggy was truly a child of Atlanta, five generations of her family having preceded her in living there. Her father was a prominent attorney who sent her to the best public and private schools. After the death of her mother during the influenza epidemic of 1919, however, she chose to drop out of Smith College to return home to keep house for her father and her brother. (Smith awarded her an honorary M. A. Degree after publication of her book.) She made her debut on March 13, 1921, and not long afterward married Berrien Kinnard Upshaw of North Carolina who deserted her within a few months. She subsequently married Marsh who had been the best man at her first wedding. They had no children.

Stephen recalled that Peggy was interested in writing as a child, writing and producing plays with her friends at their Peachtree Street home. She also enjoyed riding her pony which she often did in the company of some elderly Confederate veterans who told her of the war. In one of her rare interviews she told Mrs. Perkerson how she learned about the Civil War and got many of the ideas for her book as a child:

"I grew up when children were seen and not heard. That meant that when I was a child I had to hear a lot about the Civil War on Sunday afternoons when I was dragged hither and yon to call on elderly relatives and friends of the family who either fought in the war or lived behind the lines. I was usually scooped up onto a lap, told I didn't look like a soul on either side of the family, and ignored the rest of the afternoon while the gathering spiritedly re-fought the Civil War."

She recalled being "on bony knees, fat, slick taffeta laps, and soft, flowered laps" and that she dared not wiggle for fear of "getting the flat end of a hair brush where it would do the most good." Of all the knees, she said, she feared the cavalry ones the worst because they "had the tendency to trot and bounce and jog in the midst of reminiscences and this kept me from going to sleep."

Peggy's untimely death was the result of a tragic accident. She was struck by a speeding taxi as she and John crossed Peachtree Street on the way to a movie. She never regained consciousness and died five days later in Atlanta's Grady Hospital. After private services, she was buried in Atlanta's historic Oakland Cemetery within sight of the graves of the Confederate war heroes of whom she wrote.

Her trophies and souvenirs, along with her typewriter, portrait, and Pulitzer Prize, are preserved by the Atlanta Public Library, and a small, but comprehensive, collection of GWTW memorabilia is displayed by the Gone With The Wind Gallery on Nassau Street in downtown Atlanta.

Two questions most often asked about her were whether she left any unpublished manuscripts and whether Scarlett and Rhett ever got back together.

To the former, John before his death said there was only a rough and unfinished manuscript about the "jazz age" which predated GWTW and was lost. To the latter, Peggy always replied, "I simply don't know."

Eurith Dickinson "Ed" Rivers

(Teacher, Lawyer, Mayor, Member and Speaker of Georgia House of Representatives, Two-Term Governor. Born December 1, 1895, Center Point, Arkansas. Died June 11, 1967, Atlanta, Georgia.)

A man less able, articulate, and imaginative might have found the name Eurith Dickinson Rivers an insurmountable obstacle to political success. But Ed Rivers simply took the sum of his initials as a substitute first name, made the bow tie his symbol, and rode a silver tongue and a progressive vision of Georgia's future into two successive terms in the governor's office.

So closely did he track the philosophies of his idol, Franklin Delano Roosevelt, that his first term was known as the "Little New Deal." Had his second term not been flawed by an inability to finance the ambitious educational, welfare, and economic programs he wrote into law and the corruption of underlings, there is no telling how far he might have gone.

But he went into office known as "Bow Tie Eddie" and left office called "Asphalt Eddie" and "Pardoning Rivers," an erosion which blemished his record of giving Georgia such things as free school textbooks, a guaranteed seven-month school term, pensions for the aged, blind, and disabled, unemployment compensation, and record road-building and rural electrification programs. He never was able to recoup the public esteem with which he started and wound up his political career being the "spoiler" in the vicious 1946 governor's race in which Gene Talmadge won a county unit victory over majority-vote candidate James V. Carmichael. This contest ultimately culminated in Georgia's infamous three-governor controversy.

Rivers came to Georgia from Arkansas to study at Young Harris College where he received his A. B. Degree and married a Georgia girl. While studying law through LaSalle Extension University, he taught school in Toombs and Decatur Counties. After admission to the bar, he practiced law in Cairo until he moved to Lakeland where he was elected first mayor and then State Representative from Lanier County. His ability to speak extemporaneously on any subject in flowing, flowery, and moving rhetoric, his outgoing personality which won friends easily, and his diligent and knowledgeable legislative efforts resulted in his election as Speaker of the House of Representatives for two terms beginning in 1933.

He made his first race for governor as one of four candidates who opposed Richard B. Russell, Jr., in 1930. Although he did not make the runoff, his slashing attacks on the "schoolbook trust" caused Secretary of State George H. Carswell who did make the runoff to declare that "Russell would sell books at 10-cents each and Rivers would give them away." The free textbook issue was the one dearest to his heart as a former classroom teacher, and he pursued it relentlessly until he succeeded in making it a reality when he did become governor seven years later.

Rivers was an outspoken opponent of Gene Talmadge and his politics of race and reaction. When Rivers became a candidate to succeed Talmadge, Talmadge ran State Senate President Charles D. Redwine of Fayetteville against him in a bitter race which saw Redwine characterized in cartoons in the Atlanta newspapers as a puppet sitting on Talmadge's knee and always saying, "Me, too" and Rivers ridiculed Redwine from the stump as "Me Too Redwine." That same year Talmadge opposed the reelection of Russell as United States Senator, attacking Russell's support of FDR and his programs. Both Rivers and Russell were elected by landslides of more than sixty percent of the vote and Rivers interpreted his victory as an endorsement of the "New Deal" by Georgians and an indication of their desire to bring Georgia into the mainstream of the Roosevelt programs Talmadge had opposed during his two terms as chief executive.

The General Assembly also viewed the outcome as a mandate. Under Rivers' leadership, a flood of bills was passed in the 1937 session to implement "New Deal" programs and to plug Georgia into their benefits. The Georgia Housing Authority was created to obtain federal funds for slum clearance and public housing. The Soil Conservation Service was activated, and more than two-thirds of Georgia land was placed in the soil conservation districts established. The Rural Electrification

Program was implemented, and Georgia jumped from the bottom to the top of the states in the number of REA cooperatives.

The State Bureau of Unemployment Compensation was set up to enable Georgians to receive unemployment benefits. The State Department of Welfare was overhauled and strengthened with the requirement that each county must establish a welfare department to process all applications for aid to the aged, blind, disabled, and dependent children. The State Highway Department was reorganized to comply with federal standards, and road-building programs were greatly accelerated. Prison and educational reforms also had high priority. Rivers succeeding in getting his free textbook and minimum school term laws passed. He was hamstrung, though, in his efforts to implement rehabilitation programs for state prisoners.

Rivers made the mistake of not seeking new revenue measures to finance his programs early in his first term while his momentum was great and while he enjoyed strong public support. Once he realized that his initiatives could not be financed within the existing tax structure, he was unable to convince the legislature to act. As a result, all of his programs were seriously underfunded, and it became necessary to dismiss many patients from mental hospitals and to cut the welfare rolls. In 1939, public schools were threatened with a foreclosure that was forestalled only through the diversion of highway funds in a battle in which Rivers and his Executive Secretary, Marvin Griffin, forcibly removed the Department Director from his office.

Rivers asked the General Assembly to enact a five percent sales tax, but the lawmakers turned him down. He narrowly escaped defeat in his bid for a second term and might have lost but for the fact that his race was overshadowed by that for the United States Senate. In the latter race, Walter F. George was opposed both by Gene Talmadge and the handpicked candidate of FDR who sought to "purge" George because of his opposition to the Roosevelt scheme to pack the United States Supreme Court. Barred by the Constitution from seeking a third term, Rivers was succeeded by his old nemesis, Talmadge, who promised to restore economy in government, liquidate the state debt, and dismantle most of the Rivers programs except for old-age pensions which he embraced with a passion.

Rivers backed his protege, Ellis Arnall, whom he had

appointed Attorney General, when Arnall opposed Talmadge for a fourth term in 1942, largely on the issue of his interference with academic freedom in the University System. Rivers had expected Arnall to return the favor when his term was up in 1946, but Arnall chose instead to endorse and campaign for Carmichael, also a former legislator. Rivers ran anyway and, while running a distant third, siphoned away enough votes to assure Talmadge a county unit victory despite Carmichael's winning a popular vote majority.

His second term as governor was racked by corruption and scandal, particularly in the areas of highway contract manipulation and the sale of pardons. As a result, charges were brought against a number of his appointees and subordinates. The Atlanta newspapers were filled with accounts of the lights burning late into the nights of the last days of his second term as pardons were processed and signed by the hundreds, one going to Griffin himself who had been convicted of contempt of court in the State Highway Department.

After his "Last Hurrah," Rivers resumed the practice of law and did not again take an active role in Georgia politics, although he was considered at one time for appointment as Ambassador to Mexico by President Truman. He took satisfaction in the fact that, while he did not achieve all of his goals in dealing with the social and economic ills which plagued the state during the Great Depression, he did help make life better at a younger age for countless Georgians through the programs he was able to implement. He also was proud that, despite the legal troubles into which some of his appointees got themselves, he brought into state government many bright, able young idealists who remained in second-level managerial positions throughout state government for many years, thus assuring a continued Rivers' imprint on Georgia government for a long period after his four momentous years in the governor's office.

David Dean Rusk

(Soldier, Educator, Lawyer, Special Assistant to the Secretary of War, Deputy Undersecretary, Assistant Secretary and Secretary of State, President of the Rockefeller Foundation, Professor of International Law at the University of Georgia. Born February 9, 1909, Cherokee County, Georgia. Resides Athens, Georgia.)

Dean Rusk, the first Georgian to hold the office of Secretary of State since John Forsyth under Andrew Jackson, served longer in that position than anyone else except Cordell Hull. With the exception of the eight years of the Eisenhower Administration when he was President of the Rockefeller Foundation, he was involved in the formulation or execution of virtually every major foreign policy decision and action of the United States from the conclusion of World War II until the end of the Johnson administration in 1969.

Because of his innate modesty and intense loyalty to those he served, it is doubtful that anyone will know in his lifetime the full extent to which he was successful in achieving his goal of sparing the world the nuclear holocaust he so feared. But it is clear from the limited facts that are on the record that, in the emphasis that has been given to his role in defending the long and unpopular war in Vietnam which he personally opposed, he has not received the credit he deserves. Hopefully he will be accorded credit by historians of the future for drawing an unyielding line against Communist aggression and bringing the world to an era of, if not detentė, at least an understanding that mutual destruction is the only result that can come from either side trying to prevail over the other by force.

While he was not always right in his predictions, notably

in the case of the North Korean and Chinese intentions in starting and escalating the Korean War, he was nearly 100 percent correct in his perceptions of the correct responses, although his advice was not always taken by his superiors. He was right in many areas. For instance, in advocating the partition of Palestine and the recognition of the State of Israel, in opposing General MacArthur's recommendations to attack Mainland China and unleash Chiang Kai-shek from Formosa, and in urging expansion of the Acheson policy of containment of Communism to include the Philippines, Formosa, and Southeast Asia in the Pacific. And in doubting the wisdom and possibilities of success of the "Bay of Pigs" invasion of Cuba; in opposing air strikes and opting for a naval blockade to give Russians time and opportunity to remove their missiles from Cuba; in insisting upon wearing the Russians out at the conference table instead of going to war over access to Berlin, the building of the Berlin Wall, and the reunification of Germany.

Other areas in which he was right included supporting the unpopular United Nations military effort to end the civil war in the Congo and thus thwart Russian attempts to penetrate Africa; insisting upon an international conference to achieve neutralization of Laos; opposing the Americanization of the war in Vietnam; and, after the failure of massive military intervention by the United States, advocating the bombing halt which led to the negotiations ultimately ending the conflict after he had left office.

Rusk's approach to all problems, which some interpreted as weak and vacillating, was to consider all aspects of all options, never to paint oneself into a corner without an alternative, and always to opt for talking, even if unproductive, as opposed to confrontation. Like few of his contemporaries he understood the difference between the ideology of Communism, which he regarded as a retrogressive philosophy doomed to ultimate failure, and the historic adventurism of Russian imperialism which would take over everything its opponents did not nail down. He also correctly perceived that Chinese nationalism was a more potent force than Marxism in Asia and, although his tenure in office predated its realization, eventually would become a wedge which would divide and make enemies of the Soviet and Sino Communists.

Rusk has been known to confide to intimates that he sometimes wonders if the outcome in Vietnam would have been different had he advocated, instead of opposing, massive

155

intervention earlier when the situation might have been salvaged. But, in retrospect, he realizes he failed to persuade the American people of the importance of the effort in Vietnam as symbolic of America's role as the protector of the weak and that he overestimated both the will and capacity of the American people to pay the price of world leadership.

To understand Dean Rusk's motives and modus operandi it is necessary to understand the background of economic poverty and intellectual wealth in which he was reared.

He was the son of a Presbyterian minister who had to leave the pulpit when he lost his voice and eke out an existence for his family of seven on a red-clay farm in Cherokee County. His hard work never netted more than $100 worth of cotton and several jugs of sorghum syrup a year. As a result, Rusk grew up regarding the ultimate luxury as the monthly can of Vienna sausage his father bought and, in all his years on the diplomatic circuit, he always headed for the Vienna sausage instead of the caviar at receptions.

Rusk's mother taught him how to read and write, and his father moved the family to Atlanta to take a job as a letter carrier so Dean could get a classic education in Greek, Latin, science, and mathematics at Boy's High School. After hours he was able to supplement the family income with odd jobs like selling Coca-Cola on the streets and working as an office boy and file clerk. He worked his way through Davidson College with the help of an ROTC Scholarship and won a Rhodes Scholarship to Oxford where he had many new and exciting experiences. At Oxford he took his first drink of alcohol, was selected for a year's study in Germany, where he witnessed the early days of Hitler, and won the Cecil Peace Prize for his essay on the League of Nations. This marked the beginning of his intense and continuing interest in collective security and his unwavering support of and belief in the United Nations as such an instrument.

This background was one which Rusk used to great advantage in his future contacts with representatives of undeveloped areas, citing it in refutation of their contention that it would take their countries several centuries to catch up with the technology of the advanced nations. He told them how "in one lifetime" Georgia was transformed and insisted their people could do likewise. He also said it was his inspiration for shifting the emphasis of foreign aid from massive capital outlay projects to programs of education, health, and agricultural productivity.

He regarded himself as an embodiment of the American Dream and never missed an opportunity to point out that fact to critics and skeptics. He was a Southern liberal who was committed to the aspirations of nonwhite people around the world. And he was a universalist who believed the United States should serve as a model for the world and use the system which had rewarded him so well to meet the needs of people everywhere. To say that he was an idealist would be an understatement, but his was idealism tempered by a personal understanding of the harsh realities of life as it really is and a tough, anti-Communist patriotism committed to the Wilsonian goal of making and keeping the world safe for freedom.

He served as Dean of Faculty and taught government and international relations at Mills College while studying law at the University of California. While there he was called to active duty as a captain in the Third Infantry Division in 1940 from which he was transferred to Military Intelligence and sent to Southeast Asia where he became Deputy Chief of Staff to General Joe Stillwell. In April 1945 he was brought to the Pentagon to advise Secretary of War Henry Stimson and General George Marshall, a job in which he participated in choosing the 38th parallel as the demarcation line later to give him so much trouble in Korea.

Upon discharge he was named Assistant Director of the Division of International Security Affairs in the State Department, returned to the Pentagon as Special Assistant to Secretary of War Robert Patterson, and was remembered by Marshall when he became Secretary of State. Marshall invited him to succeed Alger Hiss as Director of the Office of Special Affairs. It was in that position that he attracted the attention of President Truman who made him personal liaison between the State Department and Clark Clifford of his staff and later wrote that Rusk was "tops in my book." He moved up rapidly to be Deputy Undersecretary and Assistant Secretary for Far Eastern Affairs under Dean Acheson. In the latter position he was Truman's principal adviser during the Korean War and became acquainted with John Foster Dulles who later was instrumental in his being elected President of the Rockefeller Foundation at the end of the Truman Administration.

Rusk was everybody's second choice to be Secretary of State in the Kennedy Administration, behind all the prima donnas like Acheson, George Kennan, Chester Bowles, and others who knew Kennedy intended to be his own Secretary of State and would never name personalities like them. Rusk never was accepted into the ranks of the Camelot jet set and often was ridiculed by the sophisticates surrounding President Kennedy. Everyone, including the President, went over and under him and meddled in the internal affairs of the State Department, but he never complained. Instead, he adhered to his strong belief that only the President was empowered to make foreign policy and that it was the responsibility of the Secretary to advise him when asked and to carry out without comment or complaint the policy once made regardless of his personal feelings. Kennedy's assassination rendered moot reports that Rusk would be replaced after 1964, and Lyndon Johnson asked him to stay on. The two became close and admiring friends, Johnson in 1968 calling him "the man who has served me most intelligently, faithfully and nobly."

Upon the conclusion of the Johnson administration, Rusk was appointed to the Samuel H. Sibley Chair of International and Corporation Law at the University of Georgia, where he works quietly today in a small professor's office and tells everyone he has "a great sense of liberation" being back in Georgia and thinks "this is where the action is." He declines to discuss the details of his momentous years as a principal in the events which shaped the world as we know it and characteristically does not respond to speculation as to whether he will leave memoirs to be published after his death.

Richard Brevard Russell, Jr.

(Lawyer, Parliamentarian, Speaker of the Georgia House of Representatives, Governor, United States Senator, President Pro Tempore of the United States Senate, Presidential Candidate. Born November 2, 1897, Winder, Georgia. Died January 21, 1971, Washington, D. C.)

The Senate of the United States is the only place in the world where one can say what he wished he had said because its procedures permit senators to indulge in stultifying claptrap, ill-advised diatribes, and inappropriate colloquies and then edit, re-write, delete, or otherwise sanitize their remarks before **The Congressional Record** is printed. One of the very few senators before or since his time who never had to avail himself of the privilege of "correcting the record" was Richard Brevard Russell, Jr., who had the intellectual and oratorical capacity to deliver even extended extemporaneous addresses grammatically and contextually perfect in the way he wanted them engraved upon the pages of history. Not only that but he also had such a thorough knowledge and total recall of the rules and parliamentary procedures of the Senate that he was never overruled on procedural matters and often was consulted by the Parliamentarian about their fine points.

Russell was a "Senator's Senator" and his reverence for the institution and that of its members for him, even those who opposed him on issues and subscribed to conflicting philosophies of government, was total and bordered on idolatry. Being a confirmed bachelor who never contemplated marriage or was ever publicly linked romantically with anyone, Russell regarded the Senate as his "life and work." He is the only senator in history to have spent more than half of his lifetime in the Senate or come more closely to dominating its character and direction for a generation.

Russell was given to working 12-hour days, cooking his own meals, washing his own socks in an austere bachelor apartment, and indulging himself only with frequent visits with his kinsmen at the Russell family home at Winder. He particularly enjoyed spending Christmases with his beloved brothers and sisters and the nieces and nephews in his hometown. In his last years after his election as President Pro Tempore of the Senate and in deference to his frail and failing health, he did agree to use the chauffeured limousine which was one of the perquisites of that office. He was the oldest son of thirteen children of the Georgia Chief Justice for whom he was named, and he was particularly close to his mother, the educated and cultured Ina Dillard Russell. At his request he was buried by her side in the family cemetery. From his earliest years Russell was a scholar, and a favorite childhood photograph shows him sitting in the yard barefoot, wearing his Sunday hat and reading a book. He was graduated from the University of Georgia School of Law at the age of twenty-one. The following year he began his prodigious political and public service career with election to the Georgia House of Representatives where he served for ten years, the last four as its "boy" Speaker.

Following a campaign in which he "wore out" a Model A Ford in a statewide automobile tour, he was elected Georgia's youngest governor in history. He was sworn in by his father at the age of thirty-three in the chaos following the Crash of 1929. After campaigning on a platform of "the 3 R's — Reorganization, Redistricting and Refinancing" — he began a momentous two years in office by cutting his own salary by $3,950. He also trimmed the state budget by twenty percent and reduced the number of state departments and agencies from 102 to eighteen. Another of his achievements was the establishment of a Board of Regents to administer a unified University System of Georgia.

Upon the death of United States Senator William J. Harris, Russell appointed the publisher of **The Atlanta Journal,** Major John S. Cohen, to warm the seat and successfully sought election in his own right in a bitterly-fought contest with Congressman Charles R. Crisp of Americus. His opponent was the son of Charles F. Crisp, who had been a distinguished Speaker of the United States House of Representatives. Charles R. Crisp had succeeded his father in office.

This was the first Georgia campaign in which the new marvel of radio became a factor, and Russell used it effectively. The principal issue was the economy, but the major point of contention was Russell's liberalism versus Crisp's conservatism. In many quarters Russell was called "the boy Bolshevik" and worse.

The Georgia wunderkind had already established a national reputation for himself with his rousing and brilliant speech seconding the nomination of Franklin D. Roosevelt at the 1932 Democratic National Convention. He went to Washington in 1933 thoroughly committed to the "New Deal" and worked assiduously for its enactment, particularly for legislation dealing with agriculture, forestry, and conservation. He served as floor manager for the Rural Electrification Act and authored the School Lunch Program Act. The latter he always regarded as his most important contribution to the country.

He was challenged for reelection by fire-eating Governor Eugene Talmadge. In one of the most volatile campaigns in Georgia political history, Talmadge branded Russell a Roosevelt puppet and blamed him for plowing under crops and slaughtering hogs. But Russell, as in all his previous races, won handily and decisively and never again faced serious opposition. In his later years when asked how it was he began his Senate career as a liberal and became its staunchest conservative at the zenith of his power, he replied, "It must have been because the times changed and I did not."

Russell broke with Roosevelt over his effort to purge his senior colleague, Walter F. George who had opposed FDR's effort to "pack" the Supreme Court. On this occasion Russell made his famous and often-quoted declaration, "I have been elected to represent and work for Georgia's interest in Washington . . . and not Washington's interest in Georgia."

He turned his major attention to becoming an expert on military matters. Russell and another Georgia colleague, Congressman Carl Vinson, emerged as two of the principal leaders and architects of America's victory in World War II. He went on to become Chairman of the combined Senate Armed Forces Committee and was the man most responsible for the development of the nation's Cold War defense establishment based upon a mix of manned bombers, nuclear missiles and submarines, and highly-mobile ground forces. It was in that capacity that he defused the explosive situation created when President Truman fired General MacArthur by holding impartial and exhaustive hearings over which he personally presided.

With the emergence of the civil rights issue, Russell became the leader and spokesman of the Southern bloc in the Senate.

To achieve what he set out to do he often resorted to skillful parliamentary maneuvering. One technique was to maintain the continuous threat of tying up the Senate and the nation through filibusters. Thus he conducted brilliant delaying and compromising actions against an array of legislation ranging from Truman's FEPC to Johnson's Public Accommodations Act. He led eighty-three days of extended debate against the Civil Rights Act of 1964, yielding only when cloture was voted, but after the measure was enacted declared, "I have no apologies to anyone for the fight that I made. I only regret that we did not prevail. But these statutes are now on the books and it becomes our duty as good citizens to live with them."

In all of the civil rights controversy, he refused to leave the Democratic Party and fought for the South's position inside rather than outside the "Party of our Fathers." He received 263 votes for the Democratic Presidential Nomination in 1948 and, as a declared active candidate in 1952, received 294 votes from twenty-seven states. It was President Truman himself who commented after the 1948 convention, "I believe that if Russell had been from Indiana or Missouri or Kentucky, he may very well have been President of the United States." This view was echoed by President Richard Nixon when he addressed a reception honoring Russell in 1970.

Russell formed a lasting friendship with Lyndon Johnson when he came to the Senate and engineered election of the Texan as Senate Majority Leader in 1953. This marked the beginning of Johnson's rise to the White House. Although they later disagreed on many things, most notably civil rights, their closeness never was strained, and Russell was Johnson's most valued adviser and confidant, particularly on military matters.

Upon the assassination of President John F. Kennedy, Johnson prevailed upon Russell to serve on the Warren Commission. This he did, despite his precarious health. At his insistence, a footnote was added to the report stating that the conclusion there was no conspiracy represented a judgment based upon the best information available. Russell refused to sign the report until that statement was added.

He also strongly advised President Kennedy against involvement in Vietnam and continued to have misgivings about the American role there. Once the large-scale American commitment was made, however, he was hawkish in advocating vigorous prosecution of the war. As he pointed out, it was his philosophy that "where the American flag is committed, I am

162

committed." He also advocated a realistic policy of recognizing and dealing with the Chinese Communists.

No American leader in any position other than the presidency ever exercised greater influence or power than did Richard Russell during his last two decades of service in the Senate. It was often said that the "only power a President has that Dick Russell doesn't is that to push the button and no President would think of pushing it without consulting with Dick Russell first."

But in the exercise of that power, Russell never forgot that his first loyalty was to the State of Georgia, and he made certain that a lion's share of military dollars were spent in Georgia. At the height of his power there were fifteen major military installations in the state with an annual combined military and civilian payroll of $1 billion.

As the result of years of heavy cigarette smoking, Russell was diagnosed as suffering from emphysema in 1958. Although he did successfully overcome a malignant lung tumor in 1969, he succumbed to the debilitating effects of emphysema two years later.

Led by President Nixon, thousands of Georgians paid their respects as his body lay in state in the Rotunda of the State Capitol, and dignitaries from throughout the Free World attended the final rites held in the family cemetery in Winder.

Quoted among the eulogies were the words Dick Russell himself had written when he was in the fourth grade: "I cannot do much to make the dark world bright, said the little star. My silver beams cannot pierce far into the gloom of the night. Yet, I am part of God's plan and I will do the best I can."

George Guest
a/k/a Sequoyah

(Silversmith, Artist, Leader and Spokesman for Cherokee Indians, Inventor of Cherokee Language Alphabet. Born approximately 1770, Taskgi, Tennessee. Died in Mexico [now Texas], March 1843.)

The word "sequoyah" (sometimes spelled without the "h" or as "sequoia" in the case of the majestic redwood trees of California) in the language of the Cherokee Indians means "possum in a poke." It was given as a nickname of derision by some of the more superstitious of those Indians to the crippled, half-breed, illiterate tribesman who invented the Cherokee language alphabet which enabled his people to become the most civilized, cultured, and best governed tribe of the American Indians.

His real name was George Guest (or Gist) which was taken from his white father, a Kentuckian sent by George Washington as an emissary to the Cherokees. He was reared by his mother who came from one of the leading Cherokee families and his uncle who belonged to the Cherokee Council. Sequoyah appeared to be a full-blooded Indian, and he was brought up in the customs of his people and trained in their hunting economy.

Early in his life, he demonstrated great skill with his hands, both in building things and in drawing pictures. He produced the pictures with brushes and paints of his own manufacture, the latter being made from berries and roots. He did not go to the missionary schools to learn to read and write English as did some of the other Cherokee boys, but chose instead to become a silversmith. Soon he was turning out works which were highly valued and much sought after. No details of his deformity are known, but it was aggravated by further injury in the Creek Campaign of 1813-14. From that time on he walked with a limp.

His interest in written language was inspired around 1800 by a manuscript taken from a captured white man. He and a friend spent much time poring over the prize in an effort to decipher it. The friend insisted that it was a magic means of communication across time and space, but Sequoyah disagreed. He maintained that it was simply a white man's invention, like the rifle, which Cherokees certainly could duplicate if they set their minds to the task. This the companion challenged Sequoyah to do, and thus began a 20-year effort which caused him to be ridiculed, threatened, burned out of his home, and banished.

But Sequoyah persisted, even visiting the classrooms of the Moravian missionary schools to see how it was done in English. His first approach was to try to devise a system of character writing like that of the Chinese or Egyptians in which each word was a separate character. It soon became apparent to him, however, that the characters were multiplying like leaves on the trees. There would be no way he or any individual ever would be able to memorize or recall all of them, he concluded.

His efforts were interpreted by some to be exercises in witchcraft. The more ignorant and superstitious of his fellow Cherokees were greatly excited and disturbed by Sequoyah and his painted symbols. As a result, they blamed him for calamities from crop failures to lost battles. They railed against him, gave him the name of derision which followed him the remainder of his life, even enlisting the aid of his wife. Neither could she understand what he was trying to accomplish. While she decoyed him from the cabin, they burned down his house and with it all the years of his work on the symbols.

About that time he did something else which added to his unpopularity. That was joining with Chief Jolly in making the treaty with Andrew Jackson which committed the Cherokees to move out of Georgia to western lands being set aside for them. With all the threats against him for that and his symbol painting, he decided he had best take himself and his work elsewhere.

With a party of 331 other Cherokees, therefore, he moved to Arkansas in 1818. Three years later he was back with his Cherokee alphabet of eighty-six characters which looked like a combination of English, Greek, Hebrew, Egyptian, and Chinese letters and characters. Some of the Cherokee elders characterized his efforts as "so many pheasant tracks criss-crossing each other in light snow." Even the great John Ross, the most literate and respected of the Cherokee leaders, dismissed him with patronizing amusement.

But this time his language had taken the phonetic approach. He had broken the Cherokee tongue into eighty-six basic sounds and assigned a character to each. This meant that any person who could memorize the syllabary and knew the Cherokee vocabulary could write because there was no need to bother with spelling or syntax. He demonstrated this idea to the Cherokee Council by taking down the testimony in a court case and then calling in his six-year-old daughter, who had not been present. She read it back perfectly. The Council's first reaction was to scoff and insist it was a trick, but the following day one of its members, Big Rattling Gourd, sought out Sequoyah. He told him that after reflecting upon the matter overnight he was convinced a written language would be good for the Cherokees and he, for one, wanted to learn it.

This marked the beginning of one of the greatest demonstrations of mass education in history. Sequoyah trained a cadre of young tutors who, in turn, held classes throughout the Cherokee Nation. Soon every child and adult was studying and committing to memory his Cherokee characters. Students who had labored two years in missionary school without learning how to write basic English were producing fluent Cherokee. The effect was to virtually close down the missionary schools. The program Sequoyah developed came close to anticipating the future course of universal education in all of America and to being the precursor to the phonics approach to teaching reading.

The Cherokee Council was so impressed that in 1824 it ordered a silver medal struck in Sequoyah's honor and made him a pension of title to a salt lick in Arkansas. In 1825 it voted to appropriate $1,500 of the nation's annuity funds for the casting of type for Sequoyah's alphabet and to buy a printing press. With the arrival of the equipment in 1828, printing of a newspaper, **The Cherokee Phoenix,** was begun. Its editor was Elias Boudinot, another Cherokee half-breed who had been sent north by the missionaries to be educated at Andover. Boudinot had returned bringing a white wife, Harriet Gold, with him, their marriage having resulted in violence and closing of the school in Cornwall, Connecticut.

About the same time there arrived a young missionary from Boston, the Reverend Samuel A. Worcester, who completed work begun earlier by another missionary on the translation of the New Testament into the Cherokee language. His subsequent arrest, conviction, and imprisonment by the State of Georgia along with Dr. Elizur Butler for being in Cherokee territory without permit caused a national furor. The sensation was heightened when John Howard Payne, author of the song "Home, Sweet Home," was arrested and expelled on similar charges and wrote newspaper articles about his experiences which were circulated throughout the world.

With the printing press, the Cherokee Council not only printed its newspaper in weekly editions but also turned out a New Testament, a hymnal, a tract on temperance, and other publications for general progress and uplift. In 1827 the Cherokees established themselves as a nation and wrote and published a constitution providing for a bicameral legislature. Another accomplishment was the dissemination of the printed word to a nearly 100 percent literate population, creating the best informed and most cohesive public opinion within any group of the nation. Emissaries sent into the area from both the Georgia State and the federal governments often found the people with whom they were conferring better informed about the issues than they were. In fact, the Cherokee Nation's press became such a potent weapon of public opinion that the Georgia State Government seized it in 1835. This was followed by occupation of Cherokee territory and the forcible removal by the federal government of the entire Cherokee nation to lands in Oklahoma in 1838. More than 4,000 of the 14,000 Cherokees who set out on the "Trail of Tears" died in one of the most shameful episodes of American inhumanity to its original inhabitants.

The Cherokees later killed all of their leaders who agreed to the relocation, including Elias Boudinot. Fortunately for Sequoyah, he had returned to the lands in Arkansas given him by the Council. By now he had become a national celebrity who was sought out by prominent people. On a visit to Washington, he had the famous portrait of himself painted which shows him wearing a flowered turban, holding a long-stemmed pipe in his mouth, and pointing one finger to his syllabary.

He later went on an expedition into what was then Mexico (now Texas) looking for a fabled lost tribe of Cherokees. He died during that journey, and the exact date and place of his burial are not known. Although his fame is based on writing, his personal diary was lost, and no autobiographical writings survived him. An interesting footnote to his life, however, is

167

that before he departed on his fatal trip, he devised a similar alphabet for the Choctaw Indians and was giving thought to doing the same for all other Indian tribes upon his return.

Sequoyah achieved in a decade for the Cherokees what it had taken the white race centuries to accomplish. No primitive people ever have enjoyed in so short a time a renaissance so pronounced and remarkable as did the Cherokees. The Sequoyah alphabet and its utilization as a tool of communication and opinion formation through the printing press had made all this possible. No other people have anything like it in their history, and it has been compared to the feat of Prometheus in Greek mythology in stealing fire from the gods and giving it to man.

Although he was born in what is now the State of Tennessee and at least three other States — Arkansas, Oklahoma, and Texas — claim him, Sequoyah lived most of his life and did most of his work in what is now the State of Georgia. The Cherokee Nation tried without success to have the State of Oklahoma named "Sequoyah" instead, but that state did place him in the National Hall of Fame as one of its two most revered citizens.

It is most fitting that the name "Sequoyah" which was given to George Guest in derision has been given subsequently to the greatest of all trees, the towering redwoods of California, as a perpetual monument to his life and accomplishments.

John Marshall Slaton

(Lawyer, twice Speaker of the House of Representatives, twice President of the Georgia Senate, twice Governor, Principal Figure in Leo Frank Case, twice candidate for U. S. Senate. Born December 25, 1866, Meriwether County, Georgia. Died January 11, 1955, Atlanta, Georgia.)

Should anyone ever write a "Georgia Profiles in Courage," a principal chapter would have to be devoted to the personal and political courage exhibited by John Marshall Slaton. For Slaton sacrificed his political future and almost lost his life to save a man he believed to be innocent from the hangman's noose.

While Georgia governors before and since have been strongly denounced by irate crowds, and some even burned or hanged in effigy, Slaton is the only chief executive who had to be protected by the State Militia from being lynched and having his home burned by a howling mob. Sixteen of the security force were injured in the melee.

Before the Leo Frank case propelled him first into international notoriety and subsequently into political oblivion, Slaton was an unlikely hero by any definition. He was more inclined to quiet scholarship and legal and parliamentary brilliance than the subject of sensational headlines.

The son of a distinguished Confederate veteran and public school superintendent, he was graduated with honors from the University of Georgia and was elected to membership in Phi Beta Kappa. He was to achieve considerable success and recognition in the practice of law in Atlanta. He became involved in Democratic politics early in his professional life and, following service as President of the Young Men's Democratic League of Fulton County, was elected to the Georgia

House of Representatives. He subsequently was elected to two terms as Speaker and then to the State Senate.

He represented Fulton, Clayton, and Cobb Counties and twice was elected President. During the latter term he succeeded to the governorship upon the election of Hoke Smith by the General Assembly to succeed Joseph M. Terrell as United States Senator. He did not seek the unexpired term, instead giving his support to former Governor Joseph M. Brown. In the regular election of 1912 he ran in his own right and was elected by a large majority over Hooper Alexander of Atlanta and Joseph Hill Hall of Macon.

As both Speaker of the House and President of the Senate, Slaton gained a reputation for "absolute impartiality in his rulings." Not one of them ever was reversed. His biographer said he "never allowed himself to lose an even poise, and never departed from absolute courtesy . . . (or) made a ruling which either side could criticize as unfair." He sought the governorship on a platform of economy in government and tax equalization and took great pride in the Tax Equalization Act which he successfully advocated. In later years, he often pointed with pride to the fact that he "cut the tax twice and yet left money in the treasury." **The Atlanta Georgian** in a lead editorial called his tax law "the greatest act of constructive statesmanship placed upon the statute books of Georgia since the days of reconstruction." The paper maintained that, through it, Slaton "established his right to be known as a GENUINELY CONSTRUCTIVE STATESMAN."

U. S. Senator Augustus O. Bacon died in office during the first year of Slaton's full term as governor. Slaton appointed William S. West of Valdosta as an interim successor while he sought the office against four other candidates — Congressman Thomas W. Hardwick, John R. Cooper, Thomas B. Felder, and G. H. Hutchins. Campaigning on the success of his tax equalization act, Slaton received a plurality of both popular and unit votes, but lost to Hardwick on the fourteenth ballot after Felder withdrew. That experience led to the enactment several years later of the law requiring a second primary when no candidate for governor or United States Senator received a majority of the county unit votes. As both governor and a senatorial candidate, Slaton supported Woodrow Wilson and his policies.

The sequence of events which culminated in Slaton's political martyrdom began on Confederate Memorial Day, two months before his inauguration for his full term as governor on June 28, 1913. On that fateful day, a 14-year-old Atlanta pencil factory worker, Mary Phagan of Marietta, was found raped and murdered in the basement of the plant. Its manager, a Jew from New York named Leo Frank, was charged with the crime. Subsequently he was convicted and sentenced to hang in a raucous trial which would have met the test of few of today's standards of impartial justice.

The judge in the case said Frank's innocence "had been proved to a mathematical certainty." Yet the attorney for a black man, Jim Conley (who was convicted of complicity in the murder and sentenced to a year on the chain gang as an accessory) later claimed Conley had confessed guilt for the slaying. The United States Supreme Court, with Justices Holmes and Hughes dissenting, upheld the conviction and the verdict.

An international furor ensued, and a national movement to save Frank arose. More than 10,000 Georgians signed a petition to Governor Slaton to spare his life; and, on June 20, 1915, two days before the scheduled date of execution and six days before the expiration of his term of office, Slaton commuted the sentence to life imprisonment, stating he was not convinced that Frank's guilt had been proved.

The virilent editorials and bloody diatribes of Thomas E. Watson had enflamed public sentiment, and Slaton was well aware of the probable consequences of his action. Before making his decision, Slaton consulted with his wife, a prominent Atlanta socialite. With her approval, he announced his decision and alerted the State Militia. The Slatons were living in their own Atlanta home, "Wingfield," while the Executive Mansion was being repaired. That night a mob of more than 5,000 marched on the site and sixteen militiamen were injured in halting and dispelling the crowd bent upon hanging the Governor and burning his home. State police maintained guard over them until the expiration of his term on June 26, 1915. At that time he and Mrs. Slaton left on a round-the-world trip while passions cooled.

Frank was transferred to the State Prison at Milledgeville where, in August, a cellmate slashed his throat. On August 16, while the Slatons were still abroad, a band of twenty-five armed men seized Frank from the prison, drove him 175 miles across Georgia, and hanged him as near as they could get to Mary Phagan's grave in Marietta. Only the entreaties of a retired judge prevented them from mutilating the body. A

171

grisly photograph of the dead man hanging from a tree is a part of the archives on the case.

Governor Slaton returned to his practice of law and lived to the ripe and active age of eighty-eight. Characteristically, he never discussed the case nor in any way attempted to defend or justify his action or to attempt to respond to the many slanders against his name. He did not write his memoirs or leave a diary to give any posthumous clue as to his thoughts about the matter. He did make one further venture into politics, seeking the U.S. Senate seat of William J. Harris in 1930. He lost every county in the state except Evans.

The final postscript of exoneration was written in March of 1982 when an 83-year-old black man, Alonzo Mann, in an effort to clear his conscience, took and passed a lie detector test in declaring that, while working as Frank's office boy, he had seen Jim Conley carrying the limp body of Mary Phagan into the factory basement on Confederate Memorial Day of 1913. He said Conley told him at the time, "If you ever mention this, I'll kill you." When Mann told his mother about it, she advised him to remain silent. And so he did until 1982.

"I believe in the sight of God that Jim Conley killed Mary Phagan to get her money to buy beer," Mann stated. "Leo Frank was innocent."

Much since has been written of the vindication of the innocence of Leo Frank and an effort to obtain a posthumous pardon for him was launched.

Nothing was written about the vindication of John Marshall Slaton's judgment and the high cost he, too, paid for doing what he believed to be right.

Hoke Smith

(Lawyer, Publisher, Democratic Leader, U. S. Secretary of the Interior, president of the Atlanta Board of Education, twice Governor, United States Senator. Born September 2, 1855, Newton, North Carolina. Died November 27, 1931, Atlanta, Georgia.)

Hoke Smith was a brilliant reformer who rode a racist horse and an alliance with the great demagogue, Tom Watson, into the Georgia governor's office. He was unhorsed in the midst of an illustrious career in the United States Senate when Watson ran against him and beat him in his "Last Hurrah." Smith made a fortune practicing law, developed **The Atlanta Journal** into a potent journalistic political force in Georgia, clipped the wings of the railroads and special-interest lobbyists at the State Capitol, ended the infamous convict-leasing system, gave Georgia prohibition, and was architect of the body of laws which effectively disfranchised black citizens of the state for almost half a century.

He attained a position of national prominence and leadership as a key figure in the election of Grover Cleveland at a time when most Southerners still were pariahs of the Civil War. As Secretary of the Interior in the Cleveland Cabinet, he was a pioneer environmentalist, promoting forest reserves and saving public lands from private exploitation. He left his permanent mark upon the nation in the form of the Smith-Hughes Act providing for vocational education and the Smith-Lever Act establishing the Agricultural Extension Service.

A descendant of a hero of the Revolution and outstanding New England educators on his father's side, Smith's single name was that of his mother's prominent North Carolina family. An intellectual prodigy, his education was received largely through tutoring from his father, a college president and university professor.

Young Smith was admitted to the bar at the age of seventeen and had a lucrative law practice underway in Atlanta before reaching his majority. His interest in ending the despicable system of convict leases stemmed from a gubernatorial appointment he received to prosecute such cases. He was Chairman of the Fulton County Democratic Executive Committee at the age of twenty, was a leader in the campaign to change the state capital to Atlanta, and served for many years as President of the Atlanta Board of Education.

He purchased **The Atlanta Evening Journal** in 1887 and published it until the turn of the century. He transformed it into a potent instrument of public opinion which later was to be denounced as one of "them lyin' Atlanta newspapers." It was Smith who hired Mrs. Rebecca Latimer Felton, the feminist crusader who later was to become the first female United States Senator, as its principal columnist. In this capacity she would join with her idol, Tom Watson, in both electing and defeating Smith in years ahead. It was largely through the support of his paper that Georgia sent a delegation pledged to Cleveland to the 1896 Convention and subsequently carried the state for him. This led to Smith's Cabinet appointment which he resigned before the next election when Cleveland refused to support Bryan as the Democratic nominee.

Smith devoted himself to building his law practice and fortune, resisting all overtures that he seek the governorship. He maintained that he could not afford the loss of income it would entail. Finally the two Tom's, Watson and Hardwick, persuaded him it was his duty to run for governor on a platform of railroad reform and black disfranchisement.

He spent thirteen months on the campaign, going into every county in the state and making hundreds of speeches. Despite the bitter and determined opposition of the railroads and big corporations, he was elected in an unprecedented landslide, polling almost twice as many votes as his four opponents combined. Two of his opponents were the father of later-to-be U. S. Senator Richard B. Russell, Jr., and Clark Howell, publisher of the rival **Atlanta Constitution.** Howell would later get his revenge by backing "Little Joe" Brown and denying Smith an endorsement term in the State House. The inauguration was a popular demonstration unparalleled in Georgia.

The General Assembly, then in session, almost immediately approved three of the measures he advocated in his inaugural address — a constitutional amendment imposing literacy and property requirements which would have the effect of removing most blacks from the voter rolls; prohibition; and expanding the scope of the Railroad Commission to include regulation of gas lines, electric power companies, and street railways. Smith was to follow up those initial successes with further legislative victories to increase appropriations for public education, restrict use of child labor, abolish the convict-leasing system, regulate lobbying, and restrict campaign contributions. He failed to get laws prohibiting railroads from giving free passes to public officials and increasing taxes on railroads operating within the state.

The constitutional amendment on voting proved more difficult to ratify than he had anticipated. This was true for two reasons: apathy and an unspoken fear that it also would disfranchise poor whites who were reluctant to admit they were illiterate. The amendment provided that voters must be able to read and explain any paragraph of the federal or state constitutions. In addition, they had to own forty acres of land or property assessed at $500. But it had the saving grace of a "grandfather clause" which provided that until 1914 anyone who had served in the United States or Confederate Armies or any of their descendants could register to vote without meeting those requirements.

The legislation was ratified by the margin of 79,968 to 40,260, effectively ending black participation in Georgia elections until after World War II and to any great degree until the historic court cases preceding the civil rights enactments of the '50's and '60's.

Smith made two political mistakes which cost him a second successive term. He refused to commute the death sentence of a political protege of Tom Watson, and he fired "Little Joe" Brown, son of Civil War Governor Joseph Emerson Brown, from the Railroad Commission.

Backed by Watson and championed by Howell and his newspaper, "Little Joe" sought the office on economic issues growing out of the Depression of 1907 and Smith's opposition to the county unit system. His campaign slogan was, "Hoke and Hunger, Brown and Bread," and he became known in the press as the "silent man of Marietta" because he refused to campaign. He promised that, if elected, he would attend to the duties of the office and "not be found running all over the State for weeks at a time and allowing the business of his office to take care of itself." Brown won by 109,806 to 98,949, and the

Constitution hailed the victory as a return to "sanity, justice and conservatism."

Smith sought vindication in 1910 and succeeded in ousting Brown despite Watson's support. Shortly after his inauguration, however, the General Assembly elected him to succeed Joseph M. Terrell as United States Senator. He submitted his resignation effective November 16, 1911, delaying it in order to insure the success of his legislative program, an act for which he was strongly criticized.

Senate President John M. Slaton succeeded him as Acting Governor and served until a Special Election could fill the unexpired term. To the surprise of no one, "Little Joe" Brown was elected. Brown again opposed Smith when he sought a full Senate term in 1914, but Smith was reelected by a two-to-one margin. He continued his distinguished service in Washington where he was a principal leader in progressive matters affecting agriculture, conservation, and education. He had been a friend of President Woodrow Wilson when the two of them had law offices in the same building in Atlanta. While he opposed some of Wilson's policies before the United States entered World War I, he vigorously supported the war effort. He broke with Wilson after the war, however, on the issue of American entry into the League of Nations without reservations.

In the Senate race of 1920, Smith was caught between Governor Hugh Dorsey and Tom Watson. Dorsey supported the League of Nations and Watson — fresh from his virulent anti-Catholic crusades which had cost his magazine its Second Class Mailing Permit during the war years — mounted a fire-eating campaign against the American Legion which paid Dorsey's entrance fee. Watson called the Legion "a gilded brigade of rich young officers" who were bent upon controlling elections and plunging America into "the brutal militarism which they practiced on your sons in the Great War." Watson, whose previous public service had been limited to one term in the House of Representatives, was the surprising winner with the support of Mrs. Felton. She was to be appointed his successor and the first woman to be Senator upon his death two years later.

Thus ended the distinguished career of Hoke Smith who was vanquished by the same sword with which he originally was the victor. He devoted the remaining years of his life to repairing the depleted family fortunes. His years of public service were among the most tumultuous in Georgia political history.

Alexander Hamilton Stephens

(Educator, Lawyer, Writer and Orator, State Legislator, Congressman [before and after secession], Vice President of the Confederacy, United States Senator [not seated], Governor of Georgia. Born February 11, 1812, Wilkes County, Georgia. Died March 4, 1883, Atlanta, Georgia.)

Had Alexander Hamilton Stephens had his way, he never would have held the office for which he is most famous — that of Vice President of the Confederate States of America. An ardent Unionist and an eloquent exponent of state's rights, he worked diligently in concert with his fellow Whigs Henry Clay and Daniel Webster to admit Texas and Oregon to statehood and to devise and seek acceptance of the Compromise of 1850.

His passionate oratory on the floor of the U. S. House of Representatives in support of national unity and understanding on one occasion prompted his seatmate, Abraham Lincoln, to write that his "old eyes were still wet with tears" after listening to "Little Aleck." With the disintegration of the Whigs, he joined the Democratic Party but spurned overtures that he seek the presidential nomination in 1860. It went instead to Stephen Douglas. It is interesting to speculate how different events might have been had it been Stephens instead of Douglas who debated slavery with his friend Lincoln in the 1860 election campaign.

When the Georgia General Assembly called a convention to act on the question of secession, Stephens was elected a delegate. He found himself in the anomalous situation of being allied in support of the Unionist position with two other articulate Georgians, Benjamin Harvey Hill and Herschel V. Johnson, both of whom he had challenged to duels earlier when he felt they had impugned his integrity.

177

Although failing to carry the vote, Stephens was chosen by the state convention to attend the convention of seceded states in Montgomery, Alabama. There he took a major role in drafting the Constitution establishing the Confederate States of America, and he and Jefferson Davis were elected its Vice President and President, respectively.

The relationship of Stephens and Davis, however, was like that of oil and water. They were in constant contention throughout the brief duration of the Confederacy over such basic matters as conscription, suspension of the writ of habeas corpus, and martial law. On these issues Stephens took progressive positions as opposed to the hard and often dictatorial line of Davis. Because of those differences Stephens spent most of the last year and a half of his tenure at his beloved home, "Liberty Hall," which is now a State Historic Site and Museum in Crawfordville, Georgia. He did go to Hampton Roads, Virginia, in February 1865 to meet with Lincoln and Secretary of State Seward in an effort to negotiate a peace settlement. That, too, came to naught because of Davis' intransigence which prolonged the conflict for another two months.

Stephens was arrested at home by federal troops while playing cards with friends and was imprisoned for six months at Fort Warren in Boston Harbor. At the intercession of General Ulysses S. Grant, President Johnson pardoned him to return home to intercede with his fellow Southerners. He would urge a course of reconciliation and acceptance of the war's results as well as education of the freed blacks for productive citizenship.

While his incarceration was considerably less harsh than that endured by Davis, the experience nevertheless further eroded his frail health and turned his hair gray at the age of fifty-three. He spent his time behind bars working on his two-volume history, **A Constitutional View of the Late War Between the States.** When published in 1868 and 1870, the work had a widespread sale throughout the world, with the result that many Southerners to this day insist that the conflict be called the War Between the States rather than the Civil War.

The State of Georgia elected him to the United States Senate in January of 1866 but the Reconstruction Congress, under the bitter domination of Charles Sumner and other radicals, refused to seat him. He did testify before the Joint Reconstruction Committee of the Congress in April. His testimony was widely reported and created considerable worldwide sympathy for the plight of the South and its people.

Stephens declined a professorship at the University of Georgia, undertook publication of an Atlanta newspaper called **The Southern Sun,** practiced law, and generally tried to regain his strength and health under the aegis of Harry and Eliza, his black body servant and cook. He had bought Harry for Eliza and directed his brother, Linton, to arrange their marriage while he was in the Congress before the Civil War.

Having always suffered from delicate health and never having weighed more than ninety pounds wringing wet, Stephens became permanently confined to a wheelchair during this period after suffering a crippling injury when a gate fell on him. It also was during this period that his hospitality and philanthrophy became legend.

He reserved a room in his house (called the "Tramp Room" by his servants) for any wayfarer in need of room and board. And his gifts sent nearly 100 boys through college. Since he ignored the fact that his resources were meager, on at least one occasion his good friend, Robert Toombs, from the neighboring town of Washington, had to bail him out of debt. He also indulged in certain whims. One was that pie was good for children. He therefore had Eliza keep a fresh pie at all times, insisting that every child who visited "Liberty Hall" eat a piece.

But even his eccentricities were humored by an adoring public which felt he could do no wrong. People flocked to his doorstep seeking help, advice, or just a friendly greeting and blessing. Surprisingly, he lost his bid for a U. S. Senate seat in 1872 to war hero John B. Gordon, but the next year was elected to the House of Representatives again. He served there until his resignation in 1882.

But his retirement was short-lived because of his desire to put an end to the politics of the "Bourbon Triumvirate" of Joe Brown, John B. Gordon, and Alfred Colquitt. After flirting briefly with the offer of the gubernatorial nomination of the Independents led by Mrs. Rebecca Latimer Felton, Stephens accepted that of the Democrats. He was elected handily despite the declaration of his friend, Robert Toombs, that he was "in his dotage." He died exactly four months after taking office on November 4, 1882, having caught cold in a chilling wind and rain in Savannah while participating in the 150th anniversary of the founding of Georgia.

More than 20,000 Georgians paid their respects as his body lay in state at the State Capitol. A hundred thousand more lined the streets to Oakland Cemetery where he was buried. He was reinterred in the front yard of "Liberty Hall" in 1893 in the shadow of his statue erected in a speech-making pose. On the side of the monument are engraved his famous words: "I am afraid of nothing on earth, or above the earth, or under the earth, but to do wrong."

His only survivor was his half-brother, Linton, who subsequently was buried beside him. As a young teacher in Madison, Stephens fell in love with one of his students. At that time he made a conscious decision that his poverty and physical condition would not permit him to marry. He moved to Liberty County to become a private tutor to the sons of the LeConte family and never again considered romance or marriage. After he became a self-taught lawyer and was admitted to the bar by the great William Harris Crawford, then sitting as judge in Stephens' circuit, his fortunes improved somewhat, but his health was never more than fair and more often was precarious.

The most interesting facet of his personality was that, despite his infirmities and poor health, he was aggressive in nature and did not hesitate to demand physical satisfaction of those whom he felt had insulted him or wronged him. He challenged at least three prominent Georgians to duels, none of whom granted him satisfaction, and was himself knifed badly by a judge who took exception to a statement Stephens had made about him. The story is told that the jurist demanded an apology and Stephens responded, "Never! Cut if you wish," and cut he did. Benjamin Harvey Hill sidestepped a challenge from Stephens by a masterful letter in which he both ridiculed and flattered Stephens, stating that if anyone doubted his courage "there is a short and easy way to test it."

Unique was a word coined to describe Stephens. His colorful character and conduct combined with his superior intellect, devotion to serving the needs of others, and total generosity, made him one of the most beloved Georgians in history. He is one of the two Georgians enshrined in the National Hall of Fame.

Two stories illustrate this dramatically.

When a delegation called on Stephens in Crawfordville to escort him by train to Atlanta for his inauguration as governor, he was followed on the train by a forlorn individual who covered his face and sat huddled in the rear of the car. Asked the identity of the man, Harry said, "That's Marse Aleck's tramp."

It turned out he was a stranger who came to Liberty Hall in

180

search of food and lodging and was invited by Stephens to stay on because he had no place else to go. When Stephens was elected governor the man was terrified about his future and asked what he was to do. Stephens replied that he would go with him to the governor's mansion. "You are to live where I live for the rest of my days," he said.

The other episode occurred during a campaign debate when Stephens was getting the better of a large and bullying opponent.

"You little runt," shouted the opponent, "I could swallow you in one gulp." To which Stephens retorted: "If you did, you would have more brains in your belly than you have got in your head."

Eugene Talmadge (Father)

(Lawyer, City Court Solicitor, County Attorney, Commissioner of Agriculture, Elected Four Times and Served Three Times As Governor. Born September 23, 1884, Forsyth, Georgia. Died December 21, 1946, Atlanta, Georgia.)

Herman Eugene Talmadge (Son)

(Lawyer, Naval Officer, Elected Three Times — Once by Legislature — As Governor, United States Senator. Born August 9, 1913, Telfair County, Georgia. Resides Henry County, Georgia.)

It has been said that Eugene Talmadge would walk a mile to get into a fight and his son, Herman, would walk a mile to stay out of one. Regardless of their personal dispositions, however, one of the two was involved to one degree or another in virtually every political fight in Georgia during more than half a century. The period referred to extended from Talmadge the Elder's election as Commissioner of Agriculture in 1927 to Talmadge the Younger's defeat as United States Senator in 1980.

Between them they gave Georgia some of the best and worst government in its history, highlighted by the forcible takeover of the governor's office by Herman and his followers in the sensational three-governor controversy. This phenomenon was precipitated by the elder Talmadge's death before assuming his fourth term of office. The duo developed a flamboyant, personalized style of political campaigning unequaled before or since.

Ole Gene, with his symbolic "red galluses," unruly forelock, dramatic gestures, and magnetic, messianic personality, commanded a fighting loyalty from his "Wool Hat Boys." The loyalty exceeded even that accorded Tom Watson by his disciples. Herman, with his intense, almost hypnotic, capacity to overwhelm any challenger with biting rejoinders and colorful hyperbole, was one of the first politicians to utilize the new medium of television to project the image he desired. As a result, he added urban support to his late father's rural base. And through appearances on "Meet The Press" and other such forums, he succeeded in establishing an identity outside Georgia.

Both father and son had an uncanny ability to dramatize issues in ways which would tap the emotions of the masses. Eugene Talmadge did it in his first campaign by challenging Commissioner of Agriculture J. J. Brown to a debate and then making him a laughing stock by identifying him with the fertilizer trusts and oil lobby to which he referred as "slick fellows from the city" and "oily boys." He made the $3 automobile tag a rallying cry and, ignoring the inherent contradiction, championed old-age pensions while opposing the rest of the New Deal.

Herman Talmadge turned his repudiation by the courts into an appeal to "the court of last resort" and won at the ballot box the governor's chair the judges had denied him. And he ran the venerable and ailing Walter F. George out of the United States Senate with his campaign against "foreign giveaways."

Both overstepped themselves at times, however. Eugene Talmadge suffered a humiliating defeat at the hands of Ellis Arnall after Talmadge's forced firing of a dean and others accused of advocating integration cost the University System of Georgia its accreditation. Herman Talmadge lost his Senate seat to the first Republican elected since Reconstruction after characterizing his denouncement by the Senate for "reprehensible" conduct involving his personal finances as a "victory."

Both Talmadges engaged in blatant racial demagoguery. This was particularly true of Eugene in his last race in which he lost the popular vote but won on county units on the strength of his promise to restore the "white primary." Herman, after successfully fending off desegregation during his years as governor, later reversed himself as Senator. At this time he began seeking black support after calling the Supreme Court decision on school integration "an accomplished fact" and he even advocated repeal of the county unit system.

Eugene Talmadge was a doctrinaire conservative who believed that the best government was the least and that individuals should solve their problems for themselves. He opposed the New Deal programs of Franklin D. Roosevelt virtually from the start. In 1936 he led an abortive movement against Roosevelt's reelection, briefly flirting with a presidential candidacy of his own.

His first two administrations were rife with controversy. He used the National Guard to remove State Treasurer George Hamilton from office after the latter refused to honor Talmadge's warrants for funds when the General Assembly adjourned without passing an appropriations bill. He also put striking textile workers behind barbed wire to break cotton mill strikes in West Central Georgia. His campaigns for the United States Senate against both Richard B. Russell, Jr., in 1936, and George in 1938, were unsuccessful. In the former he made Russell's support of the New Deal an issue, and in the latter he lost to the tremendous voter backlash against Roosevelt's effort to purge George from the Senate. He won his "Last Hurrah" against James V. Carmichael in 1946 through the county unit system which he had championed as "sacred." But he died before achieving his goal of equaling Joe Brown's record of serving four terms as governor.

Eugene Talmadge's death less than a month before he would have taken office plunged Georgia into its most traumatic governmental crisis in history. His supporters, sensing the end was near, engineered a write-in campaign for Herman in the general election. On these grounds the General Assembly proceeded to elect him governor on the basis of an obscure constitutional provision providing for it to do so in cases where "no person" had a majority of votes. Even that took some doing because the canvass of returns showed Talmadge to be running third in write-in votes behind Carmichael and tombstone salesman D. Talmadge Bowers. That problem was overcome, however, by the miraculous discovery of fifty-six additional votes from the Helena Precinct of Talmadge's home county of Telfair, votes which later were discovered to be mostly those of deceased persons who "voted in alphabetical order."

With the aid of Adjutant General Marvin Griffin, Talmadge and his unruly followers took over the governor's office in a late-night assault which Arnall, who contended the Constitution required him to remain in office until his successor was "chosen and qualified," denounced as a "coup d' etat." The office also was claimed by Lieutenant Governor Melvin E. Thompson in whose favor Arnall resigned thirteen days later. Herman Talmadge occupied the office and the governor's mansion for sixty-seven days until the Georgia Supreme Court in a five-to-two decision ruled that Arnall's interpretation was correct and, inasmuch as he had resigned, Thompson was Acting Governor. Talmadge took his case to the people and was resoundingly elected to the unexpired term of his father in 1948 and won reelection to a term in his own right by a lesser margin in 1950, both times against Thompson.

Herman Talmadge's years in office were largely progressive ones after he reneged on his promise not to impose a sales tax without a favorable vote of the people. He used the resulting flood of revenue for mammoth school, hospital, and road-building programs and to implement the Minimum Foundation Program for Education. He lost in two efforts to write the county unit system into the State Constitution but was successful in enacting a plethora of laws, including a private school amendment to the Constitution, to thwart the 1954 school desegregation decision which he repeatedly decried in fiery rhetoric.

At the end of his term Herman Talmadge was perhaps the most popular governor Georgia had ever had. Even Senator George correctly read the signs. It was clear that a seat in the Senate was Herman's for the announcing.

In Washington, he worked hard at establishing himself as an authority on agricultural programs and tax law. Until his personal problems, which included admitted alcoholism and a divorce, caused him to lose control of his financial affairs, he was highly respected by his colleagues, adding luster to his reputation by his service on the Watergate Investigating Committee.

Tomochichi

(Mico of the Yamacraw Indians. Friend and Benefactor of Sir James Edward Oglethorpe and Georgia Colonists. Born Approximately 1642, Place Unknown. Died near Savannah, Georgia, October 5, 1739.)

If anyone could lay claim to the distinction of being the charter colonist of Georgia, it would have to be Tomochichi, Mico or Chief of the Yamacraw Indians. It was Tomochichi who greeted Sir James Edward Oglethorpe and his advance party when they landed on the bluff bearing the tribe's name to lay out the site for the Settlement of Savannah. It was clear from the beginning that he was no ordinary Indian in terms of the stereotypes applied to the natives in that day. Not only was he a handsome figure of a man, standing an erect six feet at the age of ninety, but he also was an articulate, intelligent, perceptive, and dignified individual with a vision for a better future for his people achieved through alliance and cooperation with the white man.

Tomochichi and Oglethorpe hit it off from the start and became such firm and fast friends that Oglethorpe carried Tomochichi and his family and fellow chiefs to England as his guests. Georgia's founder wept when Tomochichi died and gave him a military funeral in Savannah.

With the influence and assistance of Tomochichi, Oglethorpe sought peace and friendship with the Muscogean tribes, whom the British called Creeks. On May 21, 1733, he signed a treaty with the micos of the Chehaws, Eufaulas, Cowetas, Echotas, Oconees, Oswegas, Cussetas, and Pallachuolas who responded to an invitation from Tomochichi to attend a conference at Savannah which was unprecedented in its scope and results. The treaty not only granted lands to the colony and set its boundaries but also specified the conditions for trade between the colonists and the Indians. Two provisions of the document set the prices for skins and required traders to be licensed, much to the pleasure of the Indians and to the displeasure of traders from other colonies.

Tomochichi was a great speechmaker, and Oglethorpe wrote down his words when he led a delegation of tribesmen to greet the main body of colonists upon their arrival from Charleston. After having the medicine man stroke Oglethorpe with an eagle feather and present him with a buffalo robe, Tomochichi declared: "We have come to welcome you, as I promised. I have brought you a present. This is the skin of a buffalo, which is the strongest of all beasts. Inside, you see painted the head and feathers of an eagle, which is the swiftest of all birds and flies farthest. So the English are the strongest of all people and nothing can withstand them. They have a swift and far flight like the eagle. They have flown hither from the uttermost part of the earth over the vast seas. The eagle's feathers are warm and soft and signify love. The buffalo robe is warm and signifies protection. Therefore, love and protect our little families."

Another of Tomochichi's speeches is a matter of record. It is the discourse he made when he, his wife Senauki, and his nephew and adopted son Tooanahowi were presented to King George II and Queen Carolina at Kensington Palace. Wearing the colorful red and blue robes which Oglethorpe persuaded them to wear instead of their usual skimpy native attire, all three addressed the monarchs and delighted them so that the King gave them an allowance of twenty pounds a week to pay their expenses while in England. It was on this occasion that **Gentlemen's Magazine** reported Tomochichi as stating:

"This day I see the majesty of your face, the greatness of your house, and the number of your people. . . . I am come for the good of the children of all the nations of the Upper and Lower Creeks, that they may be instructed in the knowledge of the English.

"These are the feathers of the eagle which is the swiftest of birds, and who flieth all 'round our nations. These feathers are a sign of peace in our land . . . and we have brought them over to leave them with you, O Great King, as a sign of everlasting peace."

Tomochichi's party on the trip to Britain included his brother-in-law, Mico Umpichi, and five other Chiefs — Hillispilli, Apohowtski, Stimalchi, Sentauchi, and Hinguitti. They were away from Georgia from April until December of 1734.

While abroad, Umpichi died of smallpox and was buried in full regalia in Westminster Abbey. It was on that trip that the renowned artist Willem Verelst painted the famous portrait of Tomochichi in his furs and Tooanahowi holding an eagle. Another canvas printed at the same time shows Oglethorpe presenting the Indians at the Court of St. James. The latter painting now hangs in the Smithsonian Institution in Washington, D. C. Gifts valued at more than $2,000 were given to the group, including a gold watch presented by the young Duke of Cumberland to Tooanahowi. Upon his return to Georgia, Tooanahowi insisted that the name of the island "Missoe" be changed to Cumberland which it continues to bear to this date.

Tomochichi was greatly concerned about the encroachments of the Spanish in Florida upon the Georgia Colony. He met Oglethorpe at Fort Frederica upon his return to Georgia from where he and forty warriors subsequently showed Oglethorpe the precise boundary lines the Indians had agreed upon as separating the lands of the British, Spanish, and Indians. He also arranged for Oglethorpe to meet with the Creek leaders at their great council at Coweta (or Kawita as the Indians called it) Town on the Chattahoochee River near the present location of Columbus. It was an arduous, but profitable, journey. Oglethorpe smoked the calumet (peace pipe) thus insuring the neutrality of the major Indian tribes in the coming conflict in which the British triumphed over the Spanish in the Battle of Bloody Marsh. In fact, Tooanahowi fought beside Oglethorpe in that battle, was wounded, and personally killed one of the principal Spanish captains.

Tomochichi did not live to see that day of ultimate victory, however, because he died in his village home above Savannah on October 5, 1739. Oglethorpe received the word that his old friend was on his deathbed while he was recuperating in Augusta from an injury suffered on the return trip from Coweta Town. Despite his condition, Oglethorpe hastened back to Savannah where he wept upon learning of Tomochichi's death and set about carrying out his last wishes that he be buried in Savannah among his white friends.

The Chief's body clad in the robes of his rank was rowed by boat from Yamacraw Village down the Savannah River to Savannah. Around his neck was the silver snuff box given him by Lord Percival, the Earl of Egmont, on his visit to England. General Oglethorpe, Colonels Stephens and Montaigut, and Colonists Carteret, Lemon, and Maxwell were pallbearers.

Burial was in Wright's Square. The colony's guns were fired in salute to his memory.

In 1899 the Georgia Society of the Colonial Dames of America dedicated a monument to the memory of the Indian Chief. It was a boulder brought from North Georgia and placed between the Court and Custom Houses with the following inscription: "In memory of Tomochichi, the Mico of the Yamacraws, the companion of Oglethorpe and the friend and ally of the Colony of Georgia. This stone has been placed by the Georgia Society of the Colonial Dames of America. — 1739-1899."

Perhaps the best summation of Tomochichi and the great debt Georgians owe to him were the sentences from the biographical article written by Dr. William Berrien Burroughs: "Few men of Tomochichi's day possessed his wisdom, discretion and farsightedness. . . . Without his aid and friendship, General Oglethorpe's little colony would have been annihilated or driven from the Savannah River. Whereas, with it, this isolated little band of one hundred and thirty souls has grown to be a great state. . . . "

Robert Augustus Toombs

(Lawyer, Planter, Member of Georgia House of Representatives, Member of U. S. Congress, United States Senator, Secretary of State of Confederate States of America, Brigadier General in Confederate Army, Member of Georgia Constitutional Convention of 1877. Born July 2, 1810, Wilkes County, Georgia. Died December 15, 1885, Washington, Georgia.)

Of all the principal figures of the Confederacy, none more nearly was the symbol, in death as well as in life, of the glory and good life of the Old South than was Robert Augustus Toombs.

Born with both a silver spoon and a silver tongue in his mouth, Toombs not only lived the life of luxury and privilege which is associated with the South of plantations and slavery but he also was one of its most eloquent defenders. Tall, handsome, bluff, and hearty, he was a journalist's dream, providing colorful copy for two generations of newspaper writers. The chronicle began with his early days in the Georgia Legislature and extended to his baptism as a dying man. He took this step because he did not want "young men who drift so naturally into infidelity to claim me as an unbeliever."

His escapades as a student twice caused his expulsion from the University of Georgia. His drinking probably cost him the Presidency of the Confederate States of America. His wealth permitted him to live in grand style abroad while his Confederate contemporaries languished in federal prisons. And his individualism, pride, and adherence to what he believed to be principle inspired him to be a true "Unreconstructed Rebel." As such, he gave up his civil rights rather than seek pardon and

190

take an oath of allegiance to the United States Government he had fought.

Because he was so colorful and because so much was written about him, it is difficult to distinguish the myth from the man. There can be no doubt, however, that he was a man of courage who said what he thought regardless of the consequences; nor that he was a staunch and unyielding adherent of states' rights and an outspoken exponent of conservative, fiscally-responsible government at all levels; further, that he was generous to a fault with his friends and for the causes he supported; and that his character was flawed by intemperance, particularly in his later years, and by virilent racist views of black inferiority. Because his exploits were larger than life, some of the more outrageous stories about him are skimpy in their documentation.

One tale in particular is believed now to have been a figment of Henry W. Grady's oratorical imagery of the man enhanced by the later writings of a partisan Athens journalist. The latter is the story of the Toombs Oak. Toombs is supposed to have stood under the fabled oak tree in front of the University Chapel and delivered a rival commencement address which emptied the hall of the official ceremonies. This came after his second expulsion from the school had denied his participation in the graduation exercises. While the account never was denied by Toombs, it was called a "fabrication" drawn from the "vivid imagination" of Grady by University Treasurer and Historian Augustus Hull. The great Dr. E. Merton Coulter conceded it "highly probable" that Grady originated it in some speech.

Toombs finished his undergraduate work at Union College in Schenectady, New York, which boasts of having produced the Secretaries of State of both the Confederacy and the United States. (William H. Seward also had Georgia connections and was also an alumnus of Union College and studied law at the University of Virginia.)

He served six years in the Georgia House of Representatives during the economic depression from 1838 to 1844 where his was a voice raised in defense of fiscal responsibility. After Congress required the election of U. S. Representatives by districts in 1842, he and his lifelong friend, Alexander Hamilton Stephens, were elected to Congress as Whigs where he became a respected exponent of states' rights.

In 1853 he was elected to the United States Senate where he was increasingly outspoken on the subject of states' rights.

From there he went in 1856 to Boston to make a famous speech from the platform of Tremont Temple, the headquarters of the abolitionists. With the demise of the Whigs, he and Stephens went into the Democratic Party, but split over the nominee in 1860. Toombs went with the Breckinridge faction while Stephens supported the Douglas faction. They also were on opposing sides of the secession question at the Georgia Convention. But Toombs' oratory carried the day and Georgia cast her lot with South Carolina in withdrawing from the Union. Toombs had the satisfaction of going back to Washington and personally delivering his resignation from the Senate in a final and fiery speech denouncing the federal government's encroachments upon state sovereignty.

Never a man lacking for confidence in his own abilities, Toombs believed he was best qualified to be President of the Confederacy. He, therefore, was deeply disappointed that Jefferson Davis was chosen. Later he expressed the belief to Grady that had the voting been by individual delegates instead of states he would have been the choice. However, most of his biographers agree the unspoken reason he was passed over was because of his drinking problem.

Since his friend Stephens was in line to be Vice President, Toombs had to settle for being Secretary of State, although he much would have preferred and been much more qualified to be Secretary of the Treasury. He was a constant and consistent critic of Davis and his policies from that time forth, stating that the Confederate President had "an exalted notion of his own importance." He also charged that Davis failed to capitalize on the momentum and potential credit of the first sixty days of the new nation's existence to purchase arms abroad and deal the federal government a devastating military blow. He maintained at that time that the Confederates could "whip the Yankees with cornstalks." Later he charged that conscription and Davis' desire to appoint "his West Point martinets" as officers caused the Confederacy's downfall. "Killed by West Point," he said, should be the Confederacy's epitaph.

Throughout the war, Toombs, Stephens, and Georgia Governor Joseph E. Brown kept up a steady drumbeat of criticism of Davis and the Richmond government. Saying his fellow Cabinet members were "a queer crowd and had a queer history," Toombs resigned and accepted a commission as a Brigadier General in the Confederate Army. There he came into conflict with General James Longstreet over his lack of discipline. Longstreet at one time had him arrested and virtually accused him of cowardice. After acquitting himself as a hero at Antietam, Toombs resigned when he failed to get the promotion he expected.

When the war's end came, he was in his mansion, now a state museum, in Washington, Georgia. There he got word that Yankee troops were enroute to hang him on the limbs of the large oak tree which still stands in the front yard of that house. While his wife stalled the soldiers, he fled into the woods and, supplied a horse by a neighbor, made his way to New Orleans, Cuba, France, and England. He was joined by his wife and they lived two years on the proceeds of the sale of 60,000 acres of Texas land, he quipping that "I eat about an acre a day." He came home when his daughter died and, although he conferred with President Johnson about it, he declined to take the oath of allegiance required for the restoration of his citizenship. When asked why he did not seek a pardon he declared: "A pardon? I have done nothing to ask forgiveness for and I have not pardoned them yet!"

Toombs was not further molested by the federal government, however. He resumed his practice of law and, while he could not seek or hold office, he quickly became a hero again by his outspoken opposition to "carpetbag rule" and various proposals for political and social equality for the freed slaves. He once declared in commenting on a proposal authorizing Negroes to get married, "Now, what does the Negro know about the obligations of the marriage relation? No more, sir, than the parish bull or the village heifer."

He and Stephens staunchly opposed the "New South" philosophies of the Bourbon Democrats who advocated industrialization and acceptance of the new order of things. While he accused Stephens of being in his "dotage" for accepting the governorship at an advanced age, he, nevertheless, paid off all of Stephens' debts on more than one occasion. He was so overcome upon Stephens' death that, in delivering the eulogy, he "stood sobbing for fully five minutes before he would proceed . . . (and) for almost 20 minutes his emotions were so great that he was almost unintelligible."

His final service was as a member of the Constitutional Convention of 1877 in which he was the principal figure in rewriting a document which he declared was "the handiwork of Negroes, thieves and Yankees." He was so intimately involved in the work of the convention that when the State Treasury ran out of money he personally offered to pay the salaries of the delegates. He insisted upon putting stringent provisions prohibiting state debt and boasted that, through the provisions he authored, "I have locked up the treasury and thrown the key away" — provisions which proved effective well into the mid-Twentieth Century.

Sick, widowed, and nearly blinded by cataracts, he died in his beloved home at the age of seventy-five, still regarding himself a citizen of the Confederacy. His fortune at the beginning of the Civil War was estimated at $450,000, including 113 slaves. At the last accounting before his death he had restored it to $110,000 in cash and accounts receivable, $25,000 in stocks and bonds, and considerable real and personal property. In his eulogy, Henry W. Grady called him "the most remarkable man in many respects that the South ever produced."

Carl Vinson

(Lawyer, Prosecuting Attorney, Judge, Speaker Pro Tempore of Georgia House of Representatives, Member of U. S. House of Representatives for Half Century, Chairman of House Armed Services Committee, Father of Two-Ocean Navy, American Air and Missile Power and Unified Armed Services. Born November 18, 1883, Baldwin County, Georgia. Died June 1, 1981, Milledgeville, Georgia.)

When reporters asked if he would accept President Eisenhower's reported offer of appointment as Secretary of Defense, Carl Vinson said, "Of course not, I'd rather run the Pentagon from up here." There was as much truth as humor in that response because everybody who knew anything about Washington knew that the Secretary of Defense, whoever he might be, would have to seek advance approval for whatever he might want to do from Vinson, the all-powerful Chairman of the Armed Services Committee of the U. S. House of Representatives.

Vinson was known variously as "Uncle Carl," "The Admiral," "The Swamp Fox," and "That Damned Old Dictator," depending upon who was making the reference. In fact, Vinson not only ran the Pentagon and all the generals and admirals in it, but he also probably had as much to do with building that monstrous military headquarters, in which even Chiefs of Staff have been known to get lost, as any man in either the executive or legislative branches of the federal government.

From the time he made his maiden speech in Congress in 1916 on the subject of military preparedness until he retired the undefeated champion in 1965 — after having served longer in the U. S. House of Representatives than any person before or since — he was the recognized authority on all matters of defense. Ten Presidents from Wilson to Johnson called on him for advice and assistance, and, in his post-World War II years, it was said of him as it was of his Senate colleague and counterpart, Dick Russell, that the only power a President had that he did not was that of "pushing the button" and that no President would think of doing that without consulting Vinson first. It is no exaggeration to say that the outcome of World War II could have been in doubt had it not been for Vinson's vision in pushing for a modern, two-ocean Navy in the '30's and that the Russians might have gotten further in the Cold War had it not been for his prescience about the roles of air and missile power in modern defense.

The son of a farmer who chose to jerk sodas and deliver newspapers in town rather than follow a plow, he began the practice of law in Milledgeville at the age of eighteen while still attending Mercer University Law School. He was appointed Solicitor of the Baldwin County Court at twenty-two, was elected to the Georgia House of Representatives at twenty-five, and was named Speaker Pro Tempore of that body at twenty-seven. Of his service in the latter office, a newspaper of the time reported that, "Whenever he presided, this Apollo Belvedere presented an imposing and impressive presence."

In the congressional redistricting following the 1910 Census, he was instrumental in getting Baldwin County separated from populous Bibb County (Macon) and moved from the Sixth to the Tenth District. While local resentment of the change cost him reelection to his legislative seat in the only election he ever lost, it did put him in a congressional district in which he could run and win two years later by capitalizing on rural resentment of the district by Richmond County and the City of Augusta. During the interim he served by appointment of Governor Joseph M. Brown as Judge of the Baldwin County Court.

The opportunity to run for Congress came when Thomas W. Hardwick resigned to seek the Senate vacancy created by the death of Senator Augustus O. Bacon. With the help of a secretary, campaign manager, and a driver, Vinson toured every crossroad and hamlet in the district in a rented Model-T, spending twenty hours a day making himself a familiar figure in every courthouse, schoolhouse, and church in the district. He carried all but four counties and was handily elected over three wealthy opponents to both the unexpired and full terms.

On November 3, 1914, fifteen days before his 31st birthday, he was sworn in as the nation's youngest congressman.

Vinson immediately began the practice he was to continue through the next five decades of opening his office early and working into the late night hours giving personal attention to each constituent request. He was reelected by overwhelming margins to twenty-four successive congresses, the late Judge Erwin Sibley observing, "Senators, Congressmen, Governors, Judges, Solicitors-General and various other distinguished and would-be statesmen are among the casualties of the opposition."

Aside from his work, his only interests in life were looking after his invalid wife and, after her death in 1950, enjoying the company of the sons of his longtime aides and confidants, Tillman and Mollie Snead. He also enjoyed overseeing the operation of his Baldwin County farm which he bought to "learn something about agriculture." He lived there modestly in an overseer's cottage when Congress was not in session. In Washington, he took daily two-mile walks during which he gave neighbors and strangers alike advice on gardening. It was his custom to inspect every house with a "For Sale" sign to find out what it was worth. He was a voracious reader, devouring the contents of three daily newspapers, **The Army, Navy, Air Force Journal,** all the weekly news magazines, and every history, biography, and murder mystery he could "get my hands on."

His maiden speech was a major factor in the approval of a $160-million shipbuilding program which helped ready the country for its inevitable entry into World War I. His service by appointment of President Calvin Coolidge on The Morrow Board to make a sweeping inquiry into the state of the nation's air defense resulted in legislation which he authored that created the Army Air Corps and presaged the United States becoming a major commercial and military air power.

When he became a member of the Naval Affairs Committee, he met Franklin Delano Roosevelt who was then Assistant Secretary of the Navy. The two formed a friendship which continued when FDR became President two years after Vinson assumed the committee chairmanship. They worked closely on legislation to modernize the Navy and make it, in his words, "second to none." Among this legislation was the Vinson-Trammel Act of 1934 which set the goal of 102 new ships by 1942, although he had to go over Roosevelt's head in 1940 to get the Two-Ocean Navy Bill passed. Fleet Admiral Chester W.

Nimitz later was to say, "I do not know where this country would have been after December 7, 1941, if it had not had the ships and the know-how to build more ships fast, for which one Vinson bill after another was responsible."

After World War II, Vinson introduced legislation unifying the armed forces and creating the Department of Defense and the Joint Chiefs of Staff. He became Chairman of the Armed Services Committee created to oversee the new military establishment. In that capacity he was responsible for giving the Air Force the role of developing intercontinental ballistic missiles and, during the so-called "Admiral's Revolt" — as the interservice rivalry over the relative merits of bombers versus aircraft carriers was called — his hearings and leadership were reponsible for hammering out the divisions of authority and responsibility of the services which continue to date.

Vinson fought with President Truman over his administration's defense reductions. But he pitched in to help the President restore the nation's preparedness when the Korean War broke out, and chided his colleagues for trying to fix blame for the situation. Vinson told them, "Our great need right now is to get the ox out of the ditch — not to spend a lot of time trying to find out who pushed him in." He had high personal hopes for ultimate world disarmament when people would have become more educated and communication and travel would have brought them closer together. It was his belief, however, that such a goal must be achieved through strength rather than weakness.

Although accused of being dictatorial in the handling of his committee, the tobacco-chewing teetotaler was more a compromiser and an expediter than a martinet. He believed in hammering out the details in advance, avoiding speeches, and not going over the same ground twice. He had a reputation, to the delight of the media, of deflating pompous military brass and garrulous bureaucrats with the demand that they "cut out the hemmin' and hawin' and get to the point." Persons who knew him best said the gruffness, crustiness, and abruptness attributed to him were facades, and that he actually was a warmhearted, humble man who stayed close to his fundamental beliefs. According to close observers he never spoke unless he had something to say and never allowed himself to be swayed by flattery, intimidation, expediency, or anything other than what he believed to be right. Early in his career he returned some bills sent to him for introduction by a powerful constitutent, saying, "I wear no man's collar."

He did not like to travel and seldom went more than several hundred miles from his homes in Washington and Milledgeville. The junkets and inspection trips he left to committee members and aides. He did, however, make an exception before his death at the age of ninety-seven and allowed the Navy to transport him in a special plane from Warner Robins, Georgia, to Newport News, Virginia, to attend the launching ceremonies for the world's largest and most powerful ship, the nuclear aircraft carrier named in his honor, the **USS Carl Vinson.** He declined an opportunity to speak on that day, saying "everything that needs saying has been said." The **Vinson** now is on the line with the Navy which its namesake was responsible for making "second to none." Those who knew "The Admiral" say he would be proud that the men who serve on the carrier are so impressed with it that they lovingly refer to it by the Space Age name of "The Starship."

George Walton

(Surveyor, Lawyer, Member and President of Council of Safety, Delegate to Continental Congress, Signer of Declaration of Independence, Colonel in Continental Army and Hero of Revolution, Twice Governor, Twice Chief Justice of Georgia, United States Senator, Judge. Born 1749, Prince Edward County, Virginia. Died February 2, 1804, Augusta, Georgia. Buried under Signer's Monument, Augusta, Georgia.)

Although history gives him all of the credit for self-education under Spartan conditions, Abraham Lincoln had nothing on George Walton who was doing the same thing sixty years earlier. Young Walton, as an orphan apprenticed to a carpenter, schooled himself with borrowed books by the light of a fire from the shavings of his day's work in the shop. He so impressed the man to whom he was apprenticed that he helped him borrow books, let him keep the money he earned, and released him early from his apprenticeship in order that he might seek his fortune in the world. He came to Savannah where he worked first as a surveyor with Matthew Talbot and later studied and practiced law at the age of twenty with Henry Young. One of his first clients was Edward Telfair. All three —Talbot, Telfair, and Walton — subsequently became governors of Georgia.

Short and studious, Walton was described as "good looking . . . with great earnestness and dignity of manner." He was one of the organizers of the Liberty Boys at Tondee's Tavern. He also joined with Noble Jones, Archibald Bulloch, and John Houston in calling the First Provincial Congress. He was one of the original members of the Council on Safety and one of its Presidents before Bulloch became head of Georgia's government upon the arrest of Royal Governor James Wright.

Because of his learning and writing ability, Walton was named to the Committee on Correspondence and was selected to prepare the report on the Second Provincial Congress that was printed and circulated among all Georgians. When Reverend Joachim Zubly refused to support the independence movement, Walton was chosen to replace him as one of Georgia's five delegates to the Continental Congress. At the age of twenty-seven, he was one of three, along with Button Gwinnett and Lyman Hall, who were present and signed the Declaration of Independence on July 4, 1776.

Walton came home to great acclaim. For the next year he traveled constantly between Savannah and Philadelphia, according to his biographer, "making speeches and encouraging patriots." In 1777 he married the beautiful Dorothy Camber, daughter of a prominent Tory family. Dorothy Walton refused to accompany her kin into exile in the West Indies in order to remain with her husband. Walton accepted a commission as Colonel of the First Regiment of the Georgia Militia.

Walton was critical of his co-signer, Button Gwinnett, for feuding with General Lachlan McIntosh over the strategy of the war, saying Gwinnett "like Alexander the Great, imagines himself to be lord of the earth." Nevertheless, he was active in seeking McIntosh's exile from Georgia after he fatally wounded Gwinnett in a duel. And he was responsible for circulating a letter, purporting to be from the General Assembly but later proved a forgery, opposing the return of McIntosh to fight for the liberation of the state from the British invaders.

When the British invaded Georgia, Walton and 100 men were assigned to guard the approach to the Great Ogeechee Ferry. Despite Walton's warnings, his commander, General Robert Howe, failed to defend the swamps along the approach to Savannah, contending "only a tiger could get through those jungles." As a result, the British were led through the swamps by a black woodsman named Quash Dolly and captured Savannah in a flanking attack which cost the Americans 300 casualties to fifteen for the Redcoats. Colonel Walton's troops were caught by the brunt of the attack and he was wounded in the thigh by a shot which broke the bone and felled him from his horse. He was captured, treated, and held at Sunbury.

Subsequently he was exchanged for a British Naval Captain held by the Americans.

The wound crippled him for life, and he walked with a decided limp thereafter. It is unknown whether the British knew their captive was a signer of the Declaration of Independence. Considering the relatively good treatment he received compared with the vengeance wreaked upon the properties of his co-signer, Lyman Hall, it would be logical to assume they were unaware of the great prize they had in their hands.

He proceeded to the new State Capitol at Augusta where he was elected governor by one of two rival Executive Councils set up by feuding remnants of the government that had been able to get out of Savannah. For the period of several months, he was a principal in Georgia's first "three-governor controversy," the office being claimed simultaneously by himself, John Wereat as President of the rival Council, and, of course, the Royal Governor who was back in business in Savannah.

The Walton/Wereat contention was resolved in January 1780. An Assembly elected at the call of the Council dominated by the Walton faction met in Augusta and elected Richard Howley governor along with a full slate of state officials. Walton resumed his service as one of the most active members of the Continental Congress, serving on the Treasury Board, making treaties with the Indians, and signing the Articles of the Confederation for Georgia along with Edward Telfair and Edward Langworthy. He returned to Georgia when the British were forced out, resumed the practice of law, and in 1783 was named Chief Justice of Georgia, responsible for holding court in all of its counties.

In 1789 he was elected governor and during a one-year term directed the drafting of a new State Constitution. That was followed by a term as Judge of the Eastern Judicial Circuit. In 1791 he was Chairman of the Reception Committee for the visit of President Washington to Georgia and delivered the principal address of welcome on that festive occasion.

He was named Chief Justice again in 1793 and in 1795 was appointed to the vacancy in the United States Senate created by the resignation of James Jackson who came home to fight for the repeal of the Yazoo Land Act. He did not seek election to a term in his own right. He was one of the first trustees of the University of Georgia and served in a similar capacity for Richmond Academy after establishing his home at "Meadow Garden" near Augusta. In 1799 he was named Judge of the Middle Judicial Circuit comprising the counties of Richmond,

Columbia, Jefferson, Screven, Burke, Montgomery, Washington, and Warren and served until his sudden death at the age of fifty-five on February 2, 1804.

Walton was buried with honors at Rosney near Augusta where his body remained until 1848. It was then reinterred with that of Lyman Hall under Signer's Monument which was erected in Augusta in honor of the three signers of the Declaration of Independence. (The remains of the third, Button Gwinnett, could not be found at that time, and the site of his resting place still remains unverified to date.)

His granddaughter, Octavia, attained prominence in the social and literary world as Madame LeVert and was received and entertained by royalty and leaders throughout the world. Washington Irving said of her, "Such a woman as that comes along only once in a century." An admirer in Europe once said to her, "Madame, your country has the most precious document in the world, the one your grandfather signed. Do your young people make pilgrimages to see it?" A mahogany card table which belonged to her is now a prized part of the furnishings of Georgia's beautiful new governor's mansion.

Walton's biographer, Lawton B. Evans, summed up his eventful life thusly:

"Few men in the United States have received as many honors as George Walton. He was six times elected a representative to Congress, twice Governor of Georgia, once a senator of the United States, four times judge of the Superior Court, twice the Chief Justice of the State. He was a commissioner to treat with the Indians, often in the State legislature, member of nearly every important committee on public affairs during his life. His name occurs in the State's annals for over thirty years of eventful and formative history."

Thomas Edward Watson

(Lawyer, Historian, Author, Editor, State Legislator, Populist Party Leader, Congressman, United States Senator. Born September 5, 1856, near Thomson, Georgia. Died September 26, 1922, Washington, D. C.)

By any yardstick Tom Watson would measure up as Georgia's most charismatic and intellectual politician before or since his time. But the place in history that could have been his had he been consistent and persistent in the pursuit of the progressive philosophies he championed at the height of his career was denied him. He missed the mark because he bogged down in the mire of the virilent anti-Negro, anti-Catholic, and anti-Semitic writings and rantings into which he plunged in the bitter obsessions of his later years.

It is ironic that Watson achieved his ambition to serve in the United States Senate in part because of the black voters he had wooed as a young Populist congressman on the way up. In this office, however, he died because he supported their disfranchisement. Yet he made a mark seldom achieved by a first-and-only-termer in successfully sponsoring creation of rural free delivery.

His life was a succession of contradictions and reversals of loyalties and positions which he interpreted as holding "party allegiance in subordination to my adherence to the principles of what I understand to be Jeffersonian Democracy." He truly was an individual who not only marched to a different drummer but also often was his own drummer.

There are two keys to understanding what made Watson what he was in the beginning and what he became in the end of his political career. One was the poverty he suffered in the time between his father's becoming bankrupt in the panic of 1873, which forced him to drop out of Mercer University, and his becoming one of Georgia's three most prosperous and success-ful trial lawyers of the time (the other two being Robert Toombs and Benjamin Harvey Hill). The other was the total disillusion-ment and outrage he experienced when he was voted out of Congress after only one term. He was denied a second term by Democratic Party tactics which bought black votes which were for sale with barbecues and whiskey, intimidated those which were not with physical violence and at least fifteen killings, and finished off the job by stuffing ballot boxes to the extent that in Augusta the total number of votes cast was double that of registered voters.

In the first instance, Watson developed a distrust of the Bourbon aristocracy and a disdain for the power of landed wealth. This lifelong grudge manifested itself not only in his politics but also in his private life. He once horsewhipped a wealthy planter who had beaten his brother when he worked for him as a sharecropper.

In the latter case, while he never stated it in so many words, his evolving position from advocacy of black-white voter coalitions to support of black disfranchisement evidences his conclusion that "if you can't lick 'em, join 'em" In so doing, Watson placed himself and his loyalist Populist followers in the position of exercising the balance of power between the warring factions in the Democratic Party of Georgia for almost two decades.

Red-haired and slender, Watson developed "bookish" tendencies at an early age. At fourteen he was writing original essays, poetry, prose, and speeches. His early tutor, Reverend E. A. Steed, took Tom with him when he became Professor of Latin at Mercer University and later became the model for one of the characters in Watson's novel, **Bethany.** After dropping out of college, he supported himself by teaching school and read law until he was admitted to practice by the Superior Court of Richmond County. He was twenty-one. At the time, his poverty was so acute he could not pay the admission fee of $10 and the presiding judge instructed the clerk to credit him for the amount.

The ambitious Watson did not remain poor long. Within the next fifteen years, he became noted both for winning cases and making money in a practice which carried him throughout the state. His practice was largely criminal, and his ability to sway rural juries by speaking the rural idiom made him a legend in his time. Once, while successfully defending a client on a charge of hog-stealing, he pointed to the accuser and said,

205

"I presume from what he says, that he could with all ease tell you the sex of a hog, male or female, merely by smelling of the gravy."

His travels and courtroom work impressed him with the reduced social and political status of farmers and of their need for a champion. His success having made him wealthy, he decided in 1890 to close his law practice and follow his ambition for a political career. This aspiration already had been whetted by a term in the state legislature and service as a delegate to the State Democratic Convention which nominated Governor Alfred Colquitt.

With the support of the Farmers' Alliance, Watson was elected to Congress in 1890. He got into hot water with the Democratic Party immediately when he refused to support fellow Georgian Charles F. Crisp for Speaker, seeking the office instead as the nominee of the People's Party. While he never joined the Alliance, he worked actively for its platform. During his two years in Congress, he supported the eight-hour bill, led the fight which passed the legislation requiring railroads to equip their freight cars with automatic car couplers, and made the speech which defeated the bill that would have stripped the individual states of their control of the militia.

Watson's greatest achievement came on February 17, 1893, when he secured an amendment to the Post Office Appropriation Bill requiring the Postmaster General to use $10,000 of the appropriation to experiment with the free delivery of mail to people living outside the limits of incorporated towns and cities. Postmaster General Bissell refused to implement the authority, but his successor, Postmaster General Wilson, did obey the law and operated the first experimental rural free delivery on a route in his home state of West Virginia. That was the beginning of what we know as RFD and Watson is credited with being its father. When the full program was implemented, the first official route was established in Warren County, Georgia, near Norwood.

Georgia Democrats viewed Watson and the populism he espoused as a grave threat to the future of their party's control of the state and set about to defeat him with the tactics previously described. The most heated and vicious campaigns in Georgia history followed. Watson and his supporters appealed openly for black votes and urged blacks and whites to work together to solve common economic and political problems. The contest became so enflamed at one point that Watson and his followers had to protect a black minister campaigning for him from lynching, and many of his supporters were "turned out" of churches and refused credit at stores. Watson contested the election before the House of Representatives, but his appeal was denied. When he sought to regain the seat in 1894, he again was defeated.

He returned to his home, "Hickory Hill," near Thomson where he plunged into the writing period of his life. There he turned out his two-volume **Story of France,** which was so widely acclaimed it became a text in the schools of France, and his biography of Napoleon. In addition to his novel, he also wrote **Sketches From Roman History, Waterloo Campaign, The Life and Times of Andrew Jackson,** and **The Life and Times of Thomas Jefferson.** The latter volume became a best-seller of the time and added considerably to Watson's fortune.

He also began publication of his **Weekly Jeffersonian** and the monthly **Watson's Jeffersonian Magazine.** Both papers enjoyed widespread circulation and were the forerunners of **Tom Watson's Magazine** in which he disseminated his later messages of racial and religious hate, resulting in its being barred from the U. S. mails during World War I.

Also during this period he was nominated as Vice President on the Populist Party ticket of 1896 and as President in 1904, neither candidacy achieving notable success.

Aside from the controversy and turmoil it caused, the Populist movement achieved little in Georgia because Populists and Democrats began to see who could outdo the other in anti-black sentiment. After winning fifty-three seats in the General Assembly in 1894, they went into a decline which ultimately ended the attempt to establish a viable two-party system in the State. Also leading to the demise of Populism was the fact that the Democrats adopted and enacted many of the economic reforms the Populists had espoused and embraced the cause of free silver. Watson, therefore, led his followers back into the Democratic Party, and, in alliance with Thomas W. Hardwick, successfully supported Hoke Smith for Governor in 1905 on a platform of black disfranchisement and railroad reform.

Then, in another of the interesting ironies of Watson's career, he broke with Smith in 1920 and defeated him for the United States Senate with the support of the renowned feminist and columnist for Smith's **Atlanta Journal,** Mrs. Rebecca Latimer Felton. Hardwick was elected governor in the same race and, in another quirk of fate, appointed Mrs. Felton to become the first female to sit in the United States Senate when Watson died in office in 1922.

Although Watson's biographer, Bernard Suttler, proclaimed him "a great man in everything he has undertaken," Watson's assessment of himself was that he had "not been able to do that which I set out to do" which he defined as a desire to "emulate the example of such men as Stephens and Toombs." He probably would have been consoled to know that of all the statues on the grounds of the Georgia State Capitol, his is the one which stands before the main entrance. And he would have liked the two quotations from his speeches chiseled on either side of its granite base:

"Democratic institutions exist by reason of their virtue. If ever they perish it will be when you have forgotten the past, become indifferent to the present and utterly reckless as to the future."

"Give us the fortitude which, through the cloud and gloom and sorrow of apparent failure, can see the instant pinnacles upon which the everlasting sunrise rests."

Robert Winship Woodruff*

(Philanthropist, Industrialist, Former President, Director and Chairman of the Finance Committee of the Board of Directors of The Coca-Cola Company. Born December 6, 1889, Columbus, Georgia. Resides in Atlanta and at Ichauway Plantation, Baker County, Georgia.)

A Chamber of Commerce wit once remarked that "Atlanta owes most of its prosperity to General Sherman and Coca-Cola," but he probably should have attributed it to "General Sherman and Bob Woodruff" because Robert W. Woodruff is Coca-Cola. And it has been Woodruff's vision, drive, and magnanimity that have made Coca-Cola the incalculable economic force which has generated a major portion of the progress that has transformed Atlanta into one of the coming cities of the world.

A genius of industrial concepts and merchandising techniques and a dedicated exponent of the American system of private entrepreneurship, Woodruff became President of the company at the age of thirty-three. Although retired as an active officer since 1955, at the age of ninety-three he remains the dominant personal force in the world's largest soft drink firm. One of the most powerful and diverse of all conglomerates, its interests range from wine to movies and it oversees philanthropies which rival in magnitude the budgets of many of the nations of the world. A passionate believer in anonymity, Woodruff's personal life has been the exact opposite of the advertising and publicity which have made the company's famed trademark a universally-recognized symbol of all that is the best about America. It is doubtful that anyone ever will

---

*Including Asa Griggs Candler and John Styth Pemberton

know the full scope of his numerous anonymous civic gifts and philanthropic projects.

In many respects, General Sherman's proclivity for careless use of matches had as much effect on the fortunes of both sides of Woodruff's family as it did upon the changing skyline of Atlanta. His great-grandfather, Joseph Winship, came to Georgia from Massachusetts and manufactured guns for the Confederacy until Sherman's troops burned his factory. After the war, Winship became one of the largest producers of cotton gins in the world. His paternal grandfather, George Woodruff, came to Georgia from Connecticut and built a flour mill at Columbus, Georgia, which Sherman also burned. Woodruff came back in the same business and was a millionaire before he died at ninety-one.

Robert's father, Ernest, built upon his father's fortune by marrying Emily Winship and moving to Atlanta where he took a major role in its development. He was a leader in the expansion of city transit and the establishment and development of the Trust Company of Georgia, the Atlantic Ice and Coal Corporation, the Atlantic Steel Company, and the Continental Gin Company. He was disappointed that he could not persuade Robert to finish college, sternly warning him that "it's only three generations from shirt-sleeves to shirt-sleeves." Young Bob responded, "I'll take the shirt-sleeves now, while I'm young" and proceeded to take on a series of jobs as an apprentice with the General Pipe and Foundry Company, a salesman with the General Fire Extinguisher Company, and purchasing agent for the Atlantic Ice and Coal Company.

He was making $150 a month when, at the age of twenty-two, he married Nell Hodgson of Athens, Georgia, and affiliated with the White Motor Company as a truck salesman. Thus began a career in motors that saw him rise to Vice President and Sales Manager in nine years. In 1918 he was commissioned a Captain in the Ordnance Department of the U. S. Army and rose to the rank of Major before his discharge.

Robert was only three years old when Dr. John Styth Pemberton, a native of Knoxville, Georgia, and an ex-Confederate General who commanded troops under General Joe Wheeler, concocted the formula which was to become Coca-Cola using a three-legged washpot in his backyard.

A druggist who dabbled in patent medicines, Pemberton was striving to develop a headache remedy when he hit upon the recipe of cocoa and kola nuts and other ingredients which remains secret and unduplicated to this date. Then Asa Griggs

Candler entered the picture. An up-and-coming Atlanta pharmacist, Candler, who had come to Atlanta from Villa Rica to make his fortune with $1.75 in his pocket, believed the mixture to have potential as a beverage. For a total of $2,300, Candler bought first a two-thirds interest in the formula and then outright ownership from Pemberton who died soon thereafter.

At first Candler sold the concoction exclusively in his drugstore but found it so popular that he sold the store and in 1892 formed The Coca-Cola Company. In a quarter of a century he made it the most successful soft drink in the world. He made so much money that he endowed the establishment of Emory University and its famed Hospital and served without pay as one of the most popular and successful mayors in Atlanta's history.

In 1919 Candler sold the company to a group of businessmen headed by Ernest Woodruff for $25 million in what was then the largest business transaction ever consummated in the South. He gave most of the money to his family. The financing was handled by the Trust Company of Georgia which was to become known thereafter as "The Coca-Cola Bank." Four years later Bob Woodruff was named President and began to fill the destiny over the next half century which made Coca-Cola an unequaled world economic force and Woodruff a self-made multi-millionaire, industrialist, major medical builder, philanthropist and friend, confidant, adviser, and host to Presidents and world leaders. Coca-Cola and its subsidiaries are now worth billions, and the fortunes it has generated have been major bases of the growth and prosperity experienced by the City of Atlanta in particular and the State of Georgia in general.

With the death of his friend Walter White in 1929, Woodruff also assumed the Presidency of the White Motor Company for more than a year, commuting between Atlanta and Cleveland until a successor could be found. He served as Chairman of the Board of Coca-Cola from 1939 to 1942, Chairman of the Executive Committee from 1939 to 1954, and temporarily reassumed the Presidency in 1945-46. On his retirement in 1955, he remained a Director and Chairman of the Finance Committee of the Board of Directors.

In his various roles of company leadership he was responsible for the successive decisions marking its changeover to a multi-product corporation. This included introducing the other soft drinks of the company, annexing the citrus, coffee, and wine products of the Minute Maid, Duncan Foods, and Taylor

211

Wine Companies, and branching into entertainment with the takeover of Columbia Pictures. Another of his innovations was the formation of the subsidiary, Aqua-Chem, Inc., to produce systems for seawater desalting, water pollution control, packaged steam and hot water generation, and solid waste incineration.

From the beginning of his career, Woodruff believed strongly that wealth entailed responsibilities. It was out of that conviction that his numerous philanthropies developed, particularly those contributing to the health of the people of Georgia and the South.

He first became conscious of public health needs when an elderly black retainer collapsed at his feet with a malarial seizure shortly after he purchased Ichauway Plantation in Southwest Georgia in the late 1920's. Following this experience, Woodruff ordered enough quinine for everyone in Baker County and, through a grant to Emory University, eliminated malaria, hookworm, and pellagra as health problems in that area. With his mother he worked to establish the Emily and Ernest Woodruff Foundation to minister to the health and educational needs of the South. Woodruff also directs or influences the philanthrophies of this foundation and four others which are interrelated through their growth from investments in the Coca-Cola Company, including his own Trebor Foundation.

Woodruff established the Robert Winship Memorial Clinic at Emory University in honor of his mother's father, the first private specialty clinic in the South for neoplastic diseases. He also endowed the Nell Hodgson Woodruff School of Nursing at Emory named in honor of his wife. With the late U. S. Senator Walter F. George, he worked to bring the Center for Disease Control to Atlanta and made it financially possible for Emory to donate fifteen acres of land for building the facility.

His gifts have made possible Atlanta's downtown parks, Fernbank Science Center, the Atlanta Memorial Arts Center, the Archives Building of the Atlanta Historical Society, and the purchase of Ossabaw Island by the State of Georgia. He also has made major endowments to the Atlanta University Center Complex, Tuskegee Institute, the Boys' and Girls' Clubs of America, Goodwill Industries, YMCA, YWCA, and the American Red Cross.

His greatest single philanthropy was his monumental bequest of $105 million in Coca-Cola stock to Emory University, the largest single gift in the history of American philanthropy. The bequest will give Emory $6 million per year in income and will make possible not only much new construction but also the appointment of as many as twenty Woodruff Professors and the granting of scholarships to be known as "the Woodruffs" to top students throughout the nation. The significance of this funding was stated by Dean Howard Lamar of Yale University in these words:

"Emory is perhaps the last private university in the United States to have adequate resources to set a new course for graduate education."

Age has slowed Woodruff's schedule, and he lives even more quietly than formerly, mostly on his Southwest Georgia plantation. But his interest in sharing his wealth remains undiminished as is his determination to make the world a better place for the generations who succeed him.

As a 93rd birthday present, the Board of Trustees of the Atlanta Arts Alliance voted to name the city's multi-arts complex the Robert W. Woodruff Arts Center in tribute to his many benefactions.

EPILOGUE

The biggest problem in writing this book was not identifying the GREAT GEORGIANS who should be included in such a work but rather in reducing their number to the maximum of 50 dictated by the limitations of space. In so doing I know I have omitted some of the favorites of everyone and for that I apologize. Perhaps the future will afford me the opportunity to continue the characterizations in a second volume.

My personal list of the greatest of the great was developed and refined over a period of years, beginning with my studies and research as a graduate student of history at the University of Georgia where I had the privilege of being under the tutelage of the late Dr. E. Merton Coulter, one of the greatest historians of this or any other century. Over the years I have added to and subtracted from the notes and materials I began assembling at that time and last year began the work of updating and putting them into narrative form when I concluded that Georgia's Semiquincentenary Year would be the appropriate time to publish a book embracing them.

Had space permitted I definitely would have included such other greats as Musicians Ray Charles, Johnny Mercer and Otis Redding; Poets Conrad Aiken, Byron Herbert Reece and Frank L. Stanton; Opera Singer Mattiwilda Dobbs; Writers Erskine Caldwell, Caroline Miller, Carson McCullers, Flannery O'Conner, Lillian Smith and Frank Yerby; Athletes Ezzard Charles, Fran Tarkenton, Jackie Robinson, Frank Sinkwich and Charley Trippi; Scientists and Educators Charles Herty and John and Joseph LeConte; Architect John Portman; and Folk Heros Jim Bowie, Doc Holliday and Mirabeau Lamar.

Chapters also should be written about Cabinet Members John McPherson Berrien, Howell Cobb, John Forsyth, Andrew

214

Young and Wilson G. McAdoo; U. S. Supreme Court Justices Lucius C. Q. and Rucker Lamar, James M. Wayne and William B. Woods; Georgia Supreme Court Chief Justices Logan E. Bleckley, William Henry Duckworth and Richard B. Russell, Sr.; Governors Alfred H. Colquitt, Thomas W. Hardwick, Herschel V. Johnson, Wilson Lumpkin, William J. Northern, George M. Troup and Carl Sanders; Indian Leaders Elias Boudinot, Alexander McGillivary, Mary Musgrove and John Ross; Environmentalist Eugene Odom; Conservationist Cason Callaway; Agriculturist D. W. Brooks; Educators Benjamin Mays and Lucy Craft Lanly; Humorists Bill Arp and Augustus Baldwin Longstreet; Generals Lucius Clay and Courtney Hodges; Historians E. Merton Coulter and C. Vann Woodward; Coastal Developers Howard Coffin, Alfred W. Jones and Thomas Spalding; Revolutionary War Hero Noble Wymberly Jones; and Olympic Champion Paul Anderson.

Even those lists omit names which merit inclusion, all of which stand in incontrovertible proof of the central premise of this book: that the history of our beloved State is written in the bold relief of the exciting lives and deeds of the men and women who have been and are its leaders. Georgia has produced more than its share of the great leaders of the world for the past 250 years and the observance of the anniversary of its founding is a most appropriate occasion for all Georgians to pay tribute to their contributions, the sum of which is the greatness of Georgia itself.

—ZELL MILLER

Zell Miller

Zell Miller has taught history at the University of Georgia, Emory University, DeKalb Community College, and Young Harris College.

In 1976, Miller wrote THE MOUNTAINS WITHIN ME, which describes the culture and customs of the North Georgia mountains from Miller's perspective of growing up among them. The recipient of high marks from literary critics, the book is currently in its fourth printing.

In addition, Miller has single-handedly compiled the Appalachian Archives of Georgia, a collection of books, records, cassettes, and videotapes documenting the history, life, music, and customs of the Southern Appalachian region. Noteworthy parts of the collection, which is housed at the Mountain Regional Library in Young Harris, are its large number of doctoral dissertations about the region and its 8,000-plus songs, making it one of the largest collections of traditional Appalachian music anywhere in the Southeast.

Miller has been Lieutenant Governor longer than any other person in Georgia history, having been recently elected to an unprecedented third four-year term.

He and his wife, Shirley, have two sons, Murphy and Matthew, and two grandchildren.